WIN FROM WITHIN

WIN

FROM

Build Organizational Culture
for Competitive Advantage

WITHIN

JAMES HESKETT
Foreword by John Kotter

⧉ **Columbia Business School**
Publishing

Columbia University Press
Publishers Since 1893
New York   Chichester, West Sussex
cup.columbia.edu

Copyright © 2022 James Heskett

Library of Congress Cataloging-in-Publication Data
Names: Heskett, James L., author. | Kotter, John P.,
1947– writer of foreword.
Title: Win from within : build organizational culture
for competitive advantage / James L. Heskett ; foreword by
John Kotter.
Description: New York : Columbia University Press, [2022] |
Includes index.
Identifiers: LCCN 2021021955 (print) | LCCN 2021021956 (ebook)
| ISBN 9780231203005 (hardback) | ISBN 9780231554824 (ebook)
Subjects: LCSH: Corporate culture. | Organizational behavior. |
Organizational effectiveness.
Classification: LCC HD58.7 .H477 2022 (print) | LCC HD58.7
(ebook) | DDC 658.4—dc23
LC record available at https://lccn.loc.gov/2021021955
LC ebook record available at https://lccn.loc.gov/2021021956

Cover design: Noah Arlow
Cover image: Shutterstock

For Marilyn, who took a chance

CONTENTS

Foreword, by John Kotter   ix

Acknowledgments   xi

Introduction   1

1   Culture: The Nearly Perfect Competitive Weapon   9

2   Culture Engages Employees   27

3   How Culture Drives Performance: Follow the Money   45

4   Why Some Organizations Engage Employees (and Customers) Better Than Others   71

5   How Effective Cultures Are Sustained   97

6   Culture, Engagement, and Work from Anywhere   127

CONTENTS

7 Change the Culture 141

8 Lead for Competitive Advantage Through Culture 179

*Appendix: A Robust, Culture-Based Balanced
Scorecard Audit* 211

Notes 223

Index 239

FOREWORD

JOHN KOTTER

TWO BEST-SELLING books, both at least partially inspired by Japanese successes in the 1970s—*Corporate Cultures* by Terry Deal and Allan Kennedy and *In Search of Excellence* by Tom Peters and Robert Waterman, both published in 1982—introduced the idea of corporate or organizational culture to U.S. managers. This led, later that decade, to the first flurry of activity aimed at shaping or changing corporate cultures to make them a source of strength, advantage, or improved performance. From what I observed, many if not most of these efforts produced disappointing results, and the flurry of activity calmed down. But the interest in culture remained, I suspect, because enough people intuitively concluded that culture did matter, perhaps a great deal.

Some early research showed results consistent with the culture-is-key thesis. But compared to the highly quantitative work done, for example, in the fields of strategy, business economics, and finance, the culture research did not seem nearly as rigorous. And for much of the managerial world, that is where things still stand today. Culture is probably important. But it is a very soft topic. And there is no solid evidence answering either of the two big questions: What sort of culture does help drive prosperity? And if you do not have that culture, how do you create it?

Dr. Heskett and I both disagree with the assertion that there is an absence of compelling evidence that provides at least some important answers to those two questions. He will make his case in the pages to follow. I would just add that a variety of forces are making it much more important to understand that case, even if you don't agree 100 percent with it.

Specifically, as the rate of change around most industries continues to go up, I am noticing more executives talking about culture—and for good reasons. More external change almost inevitably leads to new strategies that need to be implemented, more mergers and acquisitions, more digital transformation, and more new methodologies like Agile. In each of these cases, the right culture can make the work happen much faster and better, and the wrong culture can stall or kill the effort. So, as the speed of change increases, culture becomes even more relevant.

Heskett has been thinking about and doing studies related to culture for thirty years. His presentation here is not just one more book on culture. The manuscript is unusually thoughtful and research based. It is written by someone who clearly understands the realities and challenges of running a complex organization. His ideas need to be heard. His conclusions demand serious thought.

ACKNOWLEDGMENTS

I MIGHT never have become interested in organizational culture if it hadn't been for an early experience teaching a case at the Harvard Business School on the expert response by Johnson & Johnson's management to the potassium cyanide poisoning—leading to seven deaths—of the Company's Tylenol product on the shelves of Chicago drug stores while its CEO, James Burke, was out of the country in the fall of 1982. Burke attributed the response to a management guided by the J&J organizational culture and Credo. I'm indebted to the late Frank Aguilar and his co-author, Arvind Bhambri, who wrote the case in 1983.

Any author who accumulates experiences, material, and insights over 30 years incurs many debts to those from whom he or she has learned—academic colleagues, practitioners, and sensible and insightful friends and family. For this particular book, it started with HBS colleague John Kotter and a study of the relationship between corporate culture and performance.

John's ideas and his ways of expressing them have provided inspiration since our first work together.

As we are reminded in the book, the "team" is an important contributor to employee engagement. The "team" in my case was a group of academic colleagues who more than kept me engaged at HBS under the brand of SMIG, "the service management group." We enjoyed unusual success together in the classroom, a kind of bonding on our "field trips" to various outstanding service organizations, and a substantial published output of research and teaching materials. Earl Sasser, Len Schlesinger, Gary Loveman, Jeffrey Rayport, Tom DeLong, Tom Jones, and Roger Hallowell provided the core of a group that also included James Cash, Regina Herzlinger, Stephen Greyser, and on one memorable trip on which we had to make our own hotel room beds, Luis Huete of the IESE faculty. Two colleagues, Dan O'Brien and Dan Maher, who contributed the Critical Mass "case" to this book deserve a special shout out. The years spent working with them in executive education have passed all too quickly.

Without practitioners to both contribute and test ideas, to both "teach and learn," I would be lost. I've been fortunate to know and work with some of the best, including but certainly not limited to leaders like Ken Ackerman, Colleen Barrett, Bill Bratton, Scott Cook, Bill George, Ginger Hardage, Frances Hesselbein, Fred Hubbell, Arkadi Kuhlmann, John Morgridge, Steve Odland, Bill Pollard, Bill Strickland, Bob Walter, and Tom Watson in addition to some of the others mentioned in the book, especially the late Herb Kelleher and Jack Bogle. William Horner, Mike Tian, and Mike Trigg of WCM Investment

Management have been a source of ideas based on their practical application of concepts discussed here. Joe Wheeler co-authored a book with Earl Sasser and me that provided important evidence cited in the book.

Special thanks go to two people who strongly believed in the manuscript. Carol Franco provided the encouragement and advice that led me to Myles Thompson, Director of Publishing at the Columbia University Press. I understand why few book manuscripts get read. Publishers are bombarded with piles of them. Myles not only read mine; he could discuss it with me.

This is not my first book. As a result, I've had a range of experiences, some pretty bizarre, with various publishers. In this case, editorial and production work went smoothly, thanks to Brian Smith and his team at Columbia University Press, including Michael Haskell and Robyn Massey as well as Ben Kolstad of KGL.

Authors often give thanks to family and friends for having provided moral support, time to concentrate, and quiet. In my case, they and their friends did more than that. They contributed to the book. So thank you to Marilyn, Sarah, Charles, and Ben as well as Sue Burks and Lisa Garfinkel.

Tradition dictates that it's the author's sole responsibility for all misinformation and errors of fact. Please direct all such complaints to me.

WIN FROM WITHIN

INTRODUCTION

THE USE of *win* instead of *winning* and *build* instead of *building* on the title page of this book is appropriate for what is intended as a call to action for leaders to rethink their organizations' cultures. It reflects an argument that culture change can be achieved in the typically attenuated attention span of an organization and tenure of a leader.

Much has been said about the importance of organizational culture without much evidence to back it up. Where possible in the book, I have endeavored to back up statements with data and conclusions from the best research available, to put evidence to work in the service of exploring what has been a somewhat nebulous topic, organizational culture. For example, when available, I've cited meta-analyses of many studies rather than just one or two individual pieces of research. In the later chapters of the book, as the subject turns to leadership, I had to rely more heavily on anecdotal information. Some of it was intentional because stories are an important part of the warp and woof of organizational culture.

There is a school of thought that such examples provide flimsy or even unsuitable support on which to base an argument, that they portray what leaders say rather than what they do. The argument goes on: advice that stories and examples convey does not apply to all leaders or all situations. The context in which the advice works varies from one organization to the next. The examples of best practices may do more harm than good if misapplied. There is a tendency to overlook the full range of behaviors in which even good leaders occasionally engage, including immodest, inauthentic, self-serving, and even untrustworthy ones. Instead, the emphasis is on topics such as authentic leadership or servant leadership that typify how few leaders actually lead. Critics maintain that this kind of writing helps explain why leaders have done such a poor job of engaging employees.[1]

While recognizing the frustration of those observing little or no progress in engaging employees around the world, I believe this thinking underestimates the judgment that most leaders bring to the task of shaping and reshaping a culture. None of us are perfect. But most of us strive toward that end of the perfect-to-flawed spectrum. Further, we're not so naïve as to try to apply all of the suggestions made in books such as this one. I assume you'll select what you think will be effective in the setting where you work and lead and that in applying it, you will exhibit the kind of behaviors described here. If, on the other hand, your efforts are habitually immodest, inauthentic, or self-serving, you won't get very far, especially in dealing with an organization's culture.

Throughout the book, I have tried to identify organizations and leaders where possible. There is a risk in this. One or more of these will implode over the intermediate-term future, triggering remarks about everything from the usefulness of the book to my judgment in selecting examples. After all, one of the most-read anecdotal studies of management penned by Jim Collins was composed of just eleven organizations that met his severe criteria for firms going from good to great.[2] Even so, one of them, Circuit City, went bankrupt and was sold for parts just seven years after the publication of his book. Did it negate everything Collins had found? Did it make it less useful? No, but it generated knowing comments from the usual critics of this kind of research.

There are a limited number of examples of non-U.S. organizations and leaders in the book. The challenge of including international examples when discussing the topic of culture has been noted by so-called culturalists, those who study differences in organizational cultures around the world. They have concluded that the underlying assumptions under which employees work and leaders lead are quite different from one part of the world to another.[3] While this may be changing as a result of social networking and the extensive use of common technologies by new generations of potential leaders, it still holds true to a degree. As a result, the very foundations on which cultures are based may differ. However, there is a core of values and behaviors common to most cultures that enable organization members to manage across borders. I have addressed it elsewhere and have chosen not to take the time and space to do it again here.[4] Nevertheless, chapters 3 ("How Culture Drives Performance:

Follow the Money") and 8 ("Lead for Competitive Advantage Through Culture") have relevance for leaders around the world, with or without international anecdotes and examples.

This book focuses on the decisions and behaviors of leaders, nearly all of them CEOs. This runs the risk of generating criticism about too much emphasis on the "cult of the CEO"—giving leaders too much credit for the successes or failures of their organizations. The intent, however, is to recognize leaders at all levels in the organization who are so critical to shaping and reshaping an organization's culture.

The title of this book might imply to some that culture is an element of strategy or that cultures should be aligned with specific strategies. In an age in which long-term strategic planning is a thing of the past and agile organizations are needed to cope with frequent change, effective cultures have to be able to support several successive strategies. That's why I ask you at the outset of the book to think of an organization's culture as a platform from which all kinds of change can be executed. Organizations where this appears to be especially true are those in which large numbers of frontline employees are in direct contact with customers.

As I completed the manuscript for the book, organizations around the world were confronted with the COVID-19 pandemic. It changed the face of our daily lives and the way we work. It also provided a petri dish for a flood of research about why some firms negotiated the treacherous path through the pandemic better than others and came out on the other side in stronger competitive positions. I will predict the results. When adjusted for industry-related effects of the pandemic on performance (illustrated by the degree to which users turned to the internet and services like Zoom for teaching and meeting), they will show that those organizations that put their employees first gained long-term market share and later rewarded their shareholders handsomely. These will be the organizations that functioned more effectively when they were forced almost overnight to work remotely. They will be the organizations whose leaders were able to lead from the ranks in an atmosphere in which the lights were out in the executive suite and everyone was working under the same conditions. Marc Benioff, CEO of Salesforce, put it better than I could in an interview on CNBC when he said in May 2020, "The last ninety days were a 'quarter of trust' when we wore our values on our sleeves."[5]

Several of the values that we will see discussed, adopted, and acted on more frequently are those of diversity, inclusion, and voice, especially for those with minority backgrounds. Two forces ensure this. The first is the pressure on organizations to recognize and respond to the global demonstrations in support of social justice, fueled by criminal acts against people with minority backgrounds as well as a growing sensitivity to inequality of opportunity. The second force will be an increasing realization on the part of leaders that diversity, inclusion, and voice are good for creativity, innovation, and business in general. It is one of those rare times when idealism and pragmatism make a common cause for change. An organization's culture will determine how successful the marriage will be.

It should be clear by now that an organization's culture can be a powerful competitive weapon. Yet we rarely see or hear it referred to in that way. One possible reason is that we are reluctant to associate the ethos of the best of the human work-place experience—its servant leadership, teamwork, empathy, and satisfactions—with something as crass as competition. This line of thinking suggests that it's cynical and somehow manipulative of human behavior to do so. Those who populate winning workplaces don't tend to engage in that kind of self-analysis. One reason may be that they are busier, engaged in more meaningful work with people they enjoy working with, freer to deliver results with accountability, more productive, and even healthier than their counterparts in other organizations.

Employees, customers, partners, and communities—stake-holders of all kinds—want to win as much as investors. Winning feeds on itself (until it doesn't, as we've seen). And it's the role of leaders at all levels in an organization to create and sustain cultures that are competitive and help deliver results for all stakeholders. What's new about this notion, you ask? Couldn't we have said the same thing twenty years ago? Perhaps so, except that we are at a watershed point in business history in which new generations of more highly skilled employees are entering a workforce challenged by new technologies, more knowledgeable customers, new patterns of consumption, more complex business relationships, communities whose growing needs have to be addressed, environmental issues that demand attention now—the list goes on. Some have referred to it as the third industrial revolution, centered, among other things, around the convergence of new energy sources and systems, new communication technologies, and the sharing of resources.[6] A new generation (regardless of age) of leaders, several of them featured in this book, is ascending at just the time that several

generations of new talent raised and schooled in this industrial revolution are demanding leadership sensitive to the needs
of various stakeholders. These are leaders who recognize the
power of organizational culture, both as a means of creating
more fulfilling workplaces and as a way of achieving competitive advantage.

Chapter One

CULTURE

THE NEARLY PERFECT COMPETITIVE WEAPON

STRATEGY IS hard; culture is soft. The impact of a strategy on growth and profit can be measured, but that of a culture cannot. If you get the core values shared by everyone right, the rest will take care of itself. A strong culture helps assure good performance. To change an organization's culture requires a long time. All of these assertions have been passed around in management circles over the years. And all of them are essentially wrong.

Several years ago I was boarding a flight to give a talk when I encountered a TSA officer implementing the new policy of engaging travelers in conversation as part of the security process.

"What's your destination?" he asked.

"New York."

"Business or pleasure?"

"Business."

"What kind of business?"

"I'm giving a talk."

"Where in New York?"

"At the Oriental Mandarin Hotel," I answered, becoming a little apprehensive about whether I was being sorted out as a security risk.

"What are you talking about?" he continued, apparently oblivious to the growing line behind me.

"Organizational culture."

As he looked at me, his eyes started to glaze over and he said without much interest or enthusiasm but a touch of sarcasm, "Good luck with that."

It occurred to me during the short flight that the TSA officer's response resembled responses that I've gotten from some CEOs. While regarding it as important, too many hold mistaken views of organizational culture.

What is closer to reality is that culture is not soft. The impact of culture on profit and long-term competitive success can be quantified—a way to do it is laid out in chapter 3. Too many efforts to change a culture peter out after an initial push to identify values shared by everyone in the organization; at that point, the job of codifying a culture isn't half done. A strong culture can support good performance in some organizations but can cause poor performance in others. With the proper leadership, some kinds of culture change can be engineered in months, not years, and certainly within a CEO's tenure.

ORGANIZATIONAL CULTURE AND PERFORMANCE

An organization's mission and its culture—the shared assumptions, values, behaviors, and artifacts that determine and reflect "how and why we do things around here"—really matters. There are data to support the notion that winning cultures have a significant positive impact on profits and returns to investors.

One such study, typical of many, concluded that an equally weighted index (rebalanced every quarter) of the Fortune "100 best companies to work for"—one measure of the effectiveness of an organization's culture—produced about five percentage points of annual return more for investors than investments in broader indexes such as the Russell index of 1000 large cap companies between 1998 and 2016.[1]

CEOs by and large get the importance of the connection between an organization's performance and its culture. Eric Schmidt, a former CEO of Google, has written: "When considering a job . . . smart creatives . . . place culture at the top of the list. To be effective, they need to care about the place they work. This is why, when starting a new company or initiative, culture is the most important thing to consider . . . culture and success go hand in hand."[2]

The late Tony Hsieh, long-time CEO of the highly successful online shoe retailer Zappos.com, said: "At the end of the day, just remember that if you get the culture right, most of the other stuff—including building a great brand—will fall into place on its own."[3]

Ray Dalio, the founder and chairman of Bridgewater Associates, the world's largest hedge fund, which has reputedly made more money for investors than any other, has written in a book devoted largely to his organization's culture, that "a great organization has both great people and a great culture. Companies that get progressively better over time have both."[4]

Lou Gerstner reflected on his experiences in taking over the job of CEO at a failing IBM this way: "Until I came to IBM, I probably would have told you that culture was just one among several important elements in any organization's makeup and success—along with vision, strategy, marketing, financials, and the like. . . . I came to see, in my time at IBM, that culture isn't just one aspect of the game—it is the game."[5] Gerstner employed this philosophy in one of the largest corporate turn-arounds in U.S. business history.

For many years Ken Iverson led Nucor Steel, the minimill steel producer that transformed the industry and has earned high returns for shareholders. The company's success has been attributable in large part to the successful application of technology resulting from innovative ideas generated by both employees and customers. The late Iverson led the company until 2002 and still serves as an inspiration to the organization. He is known for attributing 30 percent of the company's success to technology and industry-leading innovation. What about the other 70 percent? He attributed that to culture.[6]

Perhaps the poster child among organizations associating an organization's performance with its culture is Southwest Airlines. Although older organizations such as 3M and IBM rose to prominence in part through their strong cultures, it was Southwest Airlines that captured the imagination of management students with its innovative personnel policies when it began operating under that name in 1971. Herb Kelleher, who built Southwest Airlines around a unique culture, believed for years that culture was the company's most potent competitive weapon. It's one that still hasn't been replicated by Southwest's

U.S. competitors, even though it has been more than forty years since the Southwest strategy was made quite clear to the world by those of us who studied it at the time.[7]

Several years ago, when I talked with Kelleher in his office at Love Field in Dallas about the relative importance of culture in Southwest's success, he commented: "At the beginning . . . the questions we asked were, 'What do we want to be? What do we want to do for the world?' . . . We wanted to be the airline for the common man. . . . We said, 'stop wasting time on five- or ten-year plans. We want to start an airline. Culture comes first; what we're about is protecting and growing people.' "[8]

Kelleher made it sound as if culture was the primary element of strategy for Southwest, at least in its early days. I'm not sure if that was his intent, but it's one way of looking at culture's role in ensuring competitive advantage.

CULTURE IS A COMPETITIVE WEAPON

A growing cadre of leaders recognizes that an effective culture combined with reasonable (not necessarily the highest) compensation fosters productivity by enabling an organization to attract and keep the best people, winning all ties with organizations competing for the same talent while also ranking highly with customers. This includes leaders of U.S. organizations (other than those whose leaders were quoted earlier) like Microsoft, T-Mobile, USAA, Publix, Genentech, Cisco, Wegmans Supermarkets, salesforce.com, Progressive, the Container Store, Starbucks, and Costco, as well as organizations in other countries

such as Cemex in Mexico, Châteauform' in France, Booking
.com in The Netherlands, and Handelsbanken in Sweden.[9]

An effective culture lowers employee defections. It also produces lower staffing costs by eliminating some recruiting and
training. One recent study concludes that a strong corporate
culture fosters better execution, reduction in agency cost, and
higher productivity and creativity.[10] Another even suggests
that by reducing stress and incentives to cheat, an organization's culture can help reduce the cost of employee fraud, which
is estimated by one panel of experts to average 5 percent of
revenues.[11]

Better talent on the front lines in contact with customers
means fewer customer defections and faster sales growth. All of
this contributes significantly to financial performance.

It is easy to ignore other ways in which culture is an effective competitive weapon. Andy Grove, the legendary leader of
Intel and always the engineer, "equated culture with efficiency, a
manual for quicker, more reliable decisions" made by colleagues
all relying on the same set of assumptions and values.[12]

Unlike many elements of strategy, an organization's culture is
hard for competitors to emulate. It operates beneath the radar,
so to speak. Organizations with legendary success like Zappos
and Disney's theme park business unit have regularly hosted
visitors in classes that explain their cultures in detail. Why? An
organization's mission and culture comprise a complex set of
elements that are next to impossible to replicate. In this world
of high-tech corporate cybersecurity and espionage, cultures
represent unique competitive weapons. *They can't be hacked.*
Even if they could be replicated, they would have to fit with

other similarly unique combinations of an organization's policies, processes, and controls.

That doesn't mean, however, that we can't learn from others about how to shape an effective culture or reshape an ineffective one.

STRONG CULTURES DON'T ALWAYS WIN

A strong culture can help assure good performance. It can also help assure bad performance. A study that John Kotter and I carried out some years ago found that organizations with strong cultures appeared to be among the biggest winners *and losers* when it came to measuring such things as growth and return on investment over the ten-year period for which we examined and analyzed data from more than two hundred U.S. firms.[13]

The dysfunctional beliefs and behaviors we found when we studied a sample of firms with strong cultures and poor performance included a tendency to assume that the practices that had produced success in the past would once again foster strong performance; a strong sense of pride that had turned to arrogance toward customers, suppliers, and others; the commonly held notion that there was little to learn from competitors or other firms regarded as leaders in their respective industries; a lack of internal support for the sharing of best practices and learning in general; and an inbred management that rejected new ideas and those who might bring them to the organization.

The message is that strong cultures can support good long-term performance, but only if they also encourage such things as personal development, learning, and innovation in support of adaptability and what has become more popularly known as organizational agility.

EFFECTIVE CULTURES ANCHOR
STRATEGIC CHANGE

Most discussions of the relationship between culture and strategy focus on the limiting effects of culture on strategy. The notion is that a culture limits the kinds of strategies that can be executed. As Edgar H. Schein has put it, "More and more management consultants are recognizing . . . that, because culture constrains strategy, a company must analyze its culture and learn to manage within its boundaries or, if necessary, change it."[14]

I see it differently. Think of it as a glass-half-full vs. a glass-half-empty view. An effective culture embodies learning, innovation, and change. Cultures centered around transparency and trust pave the way for change. In this way, culture is an enabler of an agile approach to strategy. *It makes the leadership and management of all kinds of change easier.*

There is a catchy, popular, oft-repeated view that "culture eats strategy for lunch."[15] This implies a relationship that is not helpful. Culture and strategy are not in some kind of competitive race for success. It's more useful to think of culture and strategy operating in tandem to produce competitive superiority.

Culture and strategy complement each other in the most successful organizations. For example, we'll see later how Satya

Nadella went about leading a turnaround of dysfunctional aspects of Microsoft's culture. But at the same time, he was leading a major change in strategy away from the domination of Windows software, a change made more difficult by the market share and huge wealth that Windows had produced for Microsoft. It was time for the company to begin to play catch-up to Amazon in cloud computing, and fast. The culture had to be reshaped to foster trust vs. infighting, a greater reliance on judgment vs. formal controls, and higher engagement of both employees and customers that could lead to faster and easier change—including a shift in strategy—within Microsoft. The shift to a greater emphasis on a cloud-based service strategy to take its place alongside an extremely successful Microsoft software strategy was facilitated by the simultaneous effort to address the culture—how things would be done—at Microsoft going forward.[16]

The point here is that an effective culture provides a base, a platform, from which a range of strategies can be launched and executed. It's easier to change a strategy than it is to change a culture. In a competitive era demanding, in many industries, frequent changes of strategy, any one culture needs to be designed to support a range of strategies. This lays waste to the notion that culture and strategy must be in perfect alignment at all times. The range of strategies associated with any particular culture is, however, not unlimited. For this reason, cultures and the range of strategies they are capable of supporting have to be mutually supportive.

One useful way to think about the relationship between culture and strategy is that an effective culture can provide a competitive advantage for a very long time, often much longer than any strategy. This is a particular advantage in a world in which some claim that strategy today confers only short-term competitive advantage. In her book, *The End of Competitive Advantage*, Rita Gunther McGrath argues that the management presumption that competitive advantage is sustainable creates all the wrong reflexes in a world in which the best one can hope for is "transient competitive advantage." It's a world in which, among other things, smaller, faster, more agile organizational entities marshal resources rather than own them and management-by-consensus is replaced by management governed by shared overarching beliefs.[17]

Think of an effective culture as one that provides a platform, in the high-tech sense of that word, one that is designed to foster the ability to learn, adapt, innovate, and change anything, including strategy. It is this kind of platform from which strategies with transitory competitive advantage can be developed and executed. Figure 1.1 shows this. *It describes, in a nutshell, much of what this book is about.*

Here's how to read figure 1.1. An organization's culture is the foundation for phenomena leading to two of an infinite range of outcomes, track A or track B. Both can produce strategic success. But track A is a successful strategy owing little to an effective culture. The culture itself is characterized by an authoritarian management style with today's ubiquitous mission to "be the best" at something. It may make claims to be customer-centered and emphasize employee development, but it allows only limited employee voice and gives limited support for cross-boundary (read silo) cooperation.

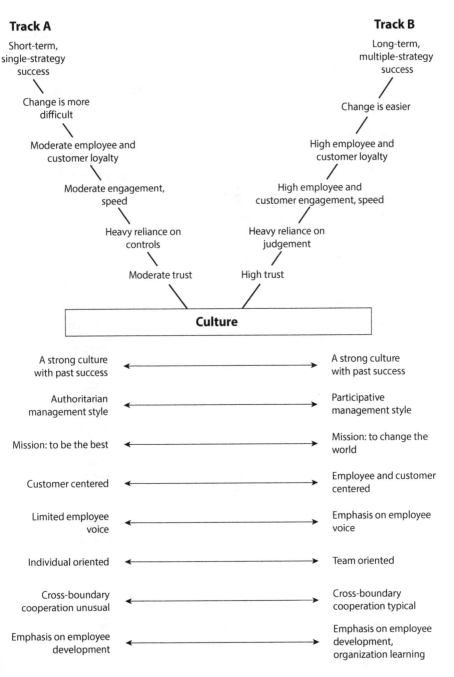

Track A

Short-term,
single-strategy
success

Change is more
difficult

Moderate employee and
customer loyalty

Moderate engagement,
speed

Heavy reliance on
controls

Moderate trust

Track B

Long-term,
multiple-strategy
success

Change is easier

High employee and
customer loyalty

High employee and
customer engagement, speed

Heavy reliance on
judgement

High trust

Culture

A strong culture with past success	←——————→	A strong culture with past success
Authoritarian management style	←——————→	Participative management style
Mission: to be the best	←——————→	Mission: to change the world
Customer centered	←——————→	Employee and customer centered
Limited employee voice	←——————→	Emphasis on employee voice
Individual oriented	←——————→	Team oriented
Cross-boundary cooperation unusual	←——————→	Cross-boundary cooperation typical
Emphasis on employee development	←——————→	Emphasis on employee development, organization learning

FIGURE 1.1 Two views of culture and strategy

As a result, organizations employing a track A culture can expect only moderate levels of trust with a relatively heavy reliance on controls to produce desired behaviors. That slows down decision making and execution. Employees and customers are loyal only to a point.

This is a culture designed to support one strategy. It may be a strategy built around a highly successful product, an effective distribution system, or even government protection. An organization may execute the strategy very well and enjoy success. But a problem presents itself when it becomes necessary to change that strategy or to make any important change in the organization. Change is very difficult. The strong, authoritarian culture makes it difficult. Success may validate the rightness of the culture—until it doesn't. But that success is relatively short for organizations on track A in a competitive environment that is changing faster and faster, much too fast for any change in culture needed to support a new strategy.

Compare this with the organization on track B in figure 1.1. It too has a strong culture, but one centered on a participative (vs. authoritarian) management style. The mission is inspirational (to change the world vs. to be the best). It is a team-oriented, employee- and customer-centered culture with an emphasis not only on employee development but also on cross-boundary cooperation and organizational learning and innovation.

The culture associated with track B fosters a high level of trust; therefore, it functions well with a heavy reliance on employee judgment (vs. more formal controls) among a group of people that is comfortable with "how and why we do things around here."

This is a place where employees like to work and are highly engaged, leading to both employee and customer loyalty that is directly linked to growth and profitability (as the numbers will show later). *This is a culture in which the leadership of change— change of any kind—is easier than most.* Ease of change extends to the matter of strategy.

A track B culture can support a range of strategies as well as a change from one to another. It is a culture geared to the long-term success of an increasingly rapidly changing panoply of strategies in an accelerating competitive environment based on a stream of new ideas and constant change. At no time has the importance of this been driven home more than during the COVID-19 global pandemic, for which no plan could be made. Agility, not long-range planning, is the answer to hard-to-predict events. Finally, effective culture is especially important for organizations in the start-up phase of their development in which several business models or strategies may have to be tested to find the one that can provide sustained success.

Repeated strategic success (and even failure for the right reasons) validates the rightness of a track B culture.

Of course, you have the option of largely ignoring issues of organizational culture. That's an interesting thing about cultures: they form with or without management intervention. But as a leader, you ignore them at your own risk. As Ben Horowitz, founder and leader of LoudCloud, a pioneer in software as a service, put it, "If you don't methodically set your culture, then two-thirds of it will end up being accidental, and the rest will be a mistake."[18]

WHAT THIS BOOK IS ABOUT

This book is about how culture contributes to great places to work and employee engagement, and how they in turn lead to profit and growth. Let's face it, organizations around the world do a lousy job of engaging their employees. Why? Much of the problem can be traced to organizational cultures that sound great and mean well until it comes to implementation. This requires an expanded view of what culture is and how it's put to work. Organizations adopting this view today have a remarkable opportunity to achieve competitive advantage. It's our concern in chapter 2.

Research tells us that this is not news to senior executives. They get it; they just don't do much about it. One of the reasons is that they can't convince themselves to put aside the firefighting, put culture change at or near the tops of their agendas, and sell the notion to their organizations. One reason is that they don't have the numbers to back it up. Chapter 3 provides the numbers and how to get them, and typically they are dramatic.

Armed with the numbers as well as the knowledge that an effective culture makes the management of all kinds of change easier, the things that sustain such a culture over time can be put in place. They include such things as self-selection of employees, organization around teams, aligning policies and practices with values and behaviors, and fostering boundary-spanning behaviors. They are described in chapters 4 and 5. In particular, attention is devoted to the matter of hiring for diversity, one concern of the social justice movement that is sweeping the globe. Research tells us that diversity is associated with certain forms of innovation. Thus, there need not be a trade-off between diversity and profit. However, as many organizations have discovered, there is no point in hiring for diversity without fostering leadership by inclusion. Those with minority backgrounds of all kinds have to have a voice. It is the responsibility of leadership to provide it.

Increasing amounts of work will be performed remotely, a trend no doubt stimulated by the COVID-19 pandemic, during which remote work was required in many parts of the world. Chapter 6 concerns the challenge of maintaining effective cultures in organizations increasingly composed especially of employees working remotely on a full-time basis.

When cultures impede performance, clearly they have to be changed—a task that many leaders dread and avoid as long as possible, often until it's too late. Chapter 7 outlines a comprehensive method for changing a poorly performing culture.

Research tells us that the single biggest determinant of an organization's culture and its impact on employee engagement is leadership. Leadership behaviors that have the greatest positive impact, along with simple devices to foster those behaviors, are discussed in chapter 8.

In writing this book, I assumed that I don't have to convince you as a leader that culture is important. You get it. You're reminded of it every day when culture is blamed in the press for scandals and disasters at companies like Boeing, Volkswagen, Wells Fargo, and Uber.

In the face of a growing body of evidence suggesting the potent competitive advantage that effective cultures can bestow, why don't more leaders act on it? It's not that CEOs deny the importance of an organization's culture. They don't. One recent comprehensive study found that 92 percent of the senior executives surveyed think that improving a firm's culture would improve its value. The problem is that the same study found that only 16 percent felt that "their firm's culture is exactly what it should be."[19] In other words, they're telling us that it's an important way to improve firm value, but 76 percent of us haven't done as much as we could to improve it.

The purpose here is to urge you as a leader to act, to give urgency to the job of reshaping an organization's culture rather than putting it at the top of a list of "nice to haves and dos." Discussions about organizational culture can seem other-worldly. But in fact, a culture contributes a great deal to an organization's ability to compete for talent, resources, and customers. Every page and topic in this book was written with this in mind.

Returning to the opening story of this chapter, I wasn't able to put the TSA officer's "good luck with that" out of my mind. What might explain it? Did it just come out automatically? Or was it prompted by something he had experienced in his TSA job? Curious, I decided to find out more about the TSA as a place to work. This is what I found: According to one rating service, TSA employees recently gave the administration a grade of D (A top to E bottom) as a place to work, placing it in the bottom 15 percent of organizations of similar size in the United States. Its thirteenth administrator or acting administrator in eighteen years was rated in the bottom 5 percent of CEOs. Employee concerns were about much more than compensation or the fast pace of work. Among other things, they rated their coworkers D+ and complained about ineffective meetings. Sixty-three percent were identified by their comments as "detractors," many of whom were not excited about going to work.[20]

So it's possible that the TSA officer's comment bore the mark of his own organization's culture. Sure, it's a sample of one. But what's the probability that it reflects the TSA's failure to engage its employees?

The most important role of culture is to contribute to a great place to work, one that engages employees in their work. So we need to understand how this is being achieved in today's most successful organizations. That is our next concern.

IF YOU REMEMBER NOTHING ELSE . . .

- Culture is hard; its impact on profit can be measured.
- An organization's culture has an impact on its productivity, sales, and costs.
- Effective cultures make all kinds of change—including efforts to change strategy—easier.
- Cultures can't be hacked.
- Strong cultures don't always win; what's needed is adaptability along with strength.
- In today's competitive environment with the need for organizational agility and constant strategic change, a culture has to be sufficiently adaptable to be able to support more than one strategy.
- Cultures form with or without management intervention. As a leader, you ignore them at your own risk.

- The primary purpose of this book is to urge you as a leader to give urgency to the task of seeking competitive advantage through culture, not just putting it at the top of the list of "nice to haves and dos." The book provides a roadmap for doing just this.

Chapter Two

CULTURE ENGAGES EMPLOYEES

EMPLOYEE ENGAGEMENT is critical to an organization's success. It yields remarkable growth and profitability, as we will see in chapter 3. One of the most important engines behind employee engagement is its culture—its shared assumptions, values, behaviors, and efforts to measure and act on them—"how and why we do things around here."

Understanding what it takes to engage employees is corporate gold. The late Tony Hsieh was a better storyteller than I am. I'll let him make the case. His Zappos.com stories are legion and choice. But my favorite of his stories concerns a time before he became CEO of the online shoe retailer, a time when, over a weekend, he and a friend Sanjay Madan created a computer program for an online advertising service eventually called LinkExchange. It grew rapidly. As Hsieh put it, "It was an exciting, fun, magical, and surreal time for all of us. We knew we were on to something big, we just had no idea how it

would turn out. All the days started blurring together. We literally had no idea what day of the week it was."[1] In the lexicon of
chapter 3, that sounds like perfection, total engagement. What
happened next is the point of the story for us.

With explosive growth, it became apparent that potential venture capitalists and even acquirers were interested in
LinkExchange. By now, the young entrepreneurs were holding
out for a sale at a company valuation of at least $250 million. But
things were changing inside the company. Back to Hsieh:

> Walking up and down the stairs of our building, I wasn't sure
> if the people I ran into worked for LinkExchange or one of
> the other companies that shared our office building. . . . It
> should have been a huge warning sign for what was to come.
> The short story is that we simply didn't know we should have
> paid more attention to our company culture. During the first
> year, we'd hired our friends and people who wanted to be
> part of building something fun and exciting. . . . Then, as
> we grew beyond twenty-five people, we made the mistake
> of hiring people who were joining the company for other
> reasons . . . motivated by the prospect of either making a lot
> of money or building their careers and resumes."[2]

It was a clear case of hiring in the absence of a clearly defined
culture that could have provided guidance to help avoid
mistakes.

Here's the punchline: LinkExchange was sold to Microsoft
for $265 million in 1998. Microsoft's offer included incentives
for the company's top three officers to stay for a year. Hsieh's

incentive amounted to 20 percent of his $40 million share of the sale price. And yet, Hsieh woke up one day and realized that "I was the co-founder of LinkExchange, and yet the company was no longer a place I wanted to be at. . . . How did things change so quickly? What happened? How did we go from an 'all-for-one, one-for-all' team environment to one that was now all about politics, positioning, and rumors?"[3] *Hsieh was no longer engaged.* He realized that he and his cofounders had failed to define the values and behaviors necessary to provide guidance in hiring those who followed. He decided to exit LinkExchange before his one-year incentive period ended, leaving $8 million on the table, and he vowed not to ignore an organization's culture again when he joined a fledgling online shoe retailer called Zappos.com.

BEGIN AT THE BEGINNING: STARTUP

Anyone who has invested in or served on the board of a startup can sympathize with Hsieh. Startups are exciting. The founders and early hires are engaged. High engagement is a given. Culture is taken for granted; it's the product of the kind of place where founders want to work. The attention is on the development of a new product or service. The next customer. Cash flow. The length of the runway needed to reach nirvana, breakeven. The business model. Finding the next investor. Hiring the next key person. Even, as Noam Wasserman puts it, dealing with the entrepreneur's ultimate dilemma of whether to be rich (sell and step aside) or be king or queen (don't sell and try to run the business).[4]

Those who are veterans of the startup experience know better than to ignore the culture and ways of sustaining employee engagement. Marc Benioff, founder and CEO of Salesforce, the leading provider of customer relationship management services, says, "Define your values and your culture up front."[5] He goes on, "We wrote down our first set of values upon the founding of Salesforce in the spring of 1999. Even as a tiny startup, we had a grand vision. . . . Our success would rest upon our ability to build a culture that adhered to our values."[6] Ellen Rubin, CEO of ClearSky Data, says, "This is my third startup, and to me and my cofounder, culture matters as much or more than our product, our marketing prowess, or our business strategy."[7]

The lesson is clear: you can have a great idea and a strategy for bringing it to market, but if you don't identify the organization's mission and establish shared values and accepted behaviors upfront, there will be no guidelines for hiring the talent needed to execute the strategy.

NEGOTIATE THE PERILOUS MIDDLE PASSAGE

The startup has succeeded. Founding managers have created the kind of place where they would like to work. The strategy has enabled rapid growth. The organization is achieving critical mass. The company is in a new industry, perhaps high-tech, in which "get big quick" is more than a prevailing notion, it is the key to survival. Talent sufficient to fuel growth has to be found. Hiring is ramped up. Whenever this happens, be aware. The time is ripe for everything from hiring mistakes to inadequate orientation for new hires. In particular, this phase of growth introduces one or more layers of middle management to the organization. Outsiders begin appearing, many with their own values and ways of doing things. Top-down and bottom-up messages begin disappearing or being altered in this new black hole of middle management. People require extra orientation, training, and follow-up, for which there is little time.

Strategy is the topic of the day. Employee engagement or deeper issues of shared values and behaviors get put aside. As a leader, you neglect culture. But, like mold, it forms anyway. It metastasizes in various ways. Behaviors are generally accepted in the marketing department that are foreign to finance. The engineers are a breed apart. People are starting to observe that things aren't the way they used to be. For one thing, no one can know everyone else, let alone know whether everyone is marching to the same beat. Newcomers form cliques in self-defense.

This is where the one-note wonders are separated from legitimate long-term survivors. It's time to stop and take stock of the organization as a place to work. Are employees engaged or not? Why? How do we know? What do we need to do to both begin measuring employee attitudes systematically and help managers at all levels engage their reports one-on-one? So our tasks may require different kinds of personalities and ways of doing things; what do we share across the organization when it comes to the way we develop our people, provide latitude for achieving results, and respect one another? Who in senior management, preferably not the already overworked human resource department, will lead this effort over time?

Writing about creating a successful startup that became a \$1 billion company in its first ten years, Marc Benioff said, "Culture needs to be continuously nurtured as the company gets bigger and ages. I consider this to be one of my more important jobs at Salesforce."[8] As an organization grows, responsibility for leading the effort to preserve its workplace quality and the engagement of its employees inevitably has to be migrated to someone with the experience, accomplishments, and the recognized authority to do the job.

BUILD TO LAST

If the rapid growth of the middle passage holds one kind of danger for the organization's culture, the slower growth of a large organization in a mature industry holds other dangers. Here, the task is one of maintaining ways of expanding jobs, opening channels for promotion, and encouraging personal on-the-job employee growth in general. Education, training, and creative organizational forms may be needed. Again, the role of middle management in this effort becomes critical. An important element of leadership is that of ensuring that pride in the mission and success of the organization doesn't morph into arrogance toward others, particularly customers. The symptoms of decline are described in greater detail at the outset of chapter 7. It's time to revisit shared values and behaviors to foster employees' engagement in the importance and quality of their work. This is what leaders of companies that are "built to last" do, as Jim Collins and Jerry Porras reminded us years ago.[9]

EMPLOYEE ENGAGEMENT—CENTRAL TO A PROFIT MODEL

Employee engagement is a person's passion for the job, the organization, and its mission. These are people who are "highly involved in and enthusiastic about their work and workplace," as the Gallup organization defines it.[10] It has become a popular concept.

Most major organizations conduct periodic employee engagement surveys in which many things are measured. In the study described in chapter 3, my subject company, MarketCo, utilizes an employee engagement index. It comprises a composite of employee responses to six statements: (1) I would recommend my company as a great place to work. (2) I intend to stay with my company for at least another twelve months. (3) My colleagues are willing to go beyond what is expected for the success of my company. (4) I am proud to work for my company. (5) My colleagues are passionate about providing exceptional customer service. (6) I understand how my job contributes to the success of my company. That's a good start. But other measures tell a more complete story of organizational health. They include such things as willingness on the job to put the organization's interests before one's own, willingness to refer potential employees (often with similar values and behaviors) to the organization, involvement in improving processes, and even suggesting new products and services.

LEADERS UNDERSTAND BUT IGNORE
ENGAGEMENT AT THEIR RISK

Successful entrepreneurs and leaders of larger organizations understand the importance of employee engagement. But apparently, few are moved to do something about it. According to a study by the Deloitte organization, 80 percent of executives around the world rated employee experience important or very important. Employee experience drives engagement. And yet in the Deloitte study, only 22 percent felt that their companies were excellent at building a differentiated employee experience.[11]

Organizations around the globe are doing a poor job of developing employees who are engaged in their work. Worse yet, even though ample research suggests how to do it, the number of actively disengaged employees far exceeds those who are engaged. And the numbers aren't improving. This is puzzling, because employee engagement may be the most effective competitive strategy available to many organizations.

The Gallup organization reports that its multinational meta-analysis of studies of employee engagement encompassing hundreds of thousands of employees in 155 countries during the 2014–2016 period showed that only 15 percent of employees were engaged according to the definition presented earlier. Two-thirds were not engaged, and 18 percent were "actively disengaged." In 2017, the rate of engagement ranged from 10 percent in Western Europe to 27 percent in Latin America and 31 percent in the United States and Canada.[12] But here's the downside: globally, those employees who are engaged are outnumbered by those who are actively disengaged and likely to be at odds with an organization, its objectives, its values, and the reasons for doing things the way it does. Worse yet, these engagement percentages fall far short of the 79 percent (in this study) who said that engagement is "very important" to their organizations.

Engaged employees are most often found in great places to work. So the basic question is: How do we create a great place to work, one that fosters employee engagement?

HOW DO WE CREATE A GREAT PLACE TO WORK?

The answer to this question is subjective; it varies from one employee to the next. But research tells us that the most important contributors to great places to work are leadership, mission, nature of the job, the team, and an effective culture, as shown in figure 2.1.

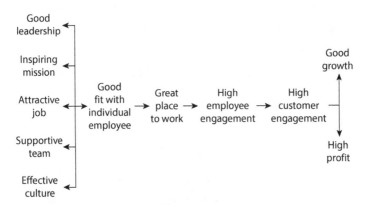

FIGURE 2.1 How culture and employee engagement contribute to profit

One of these appears to outweigh all the rest—leadership. According to one estimate by Gallup, "At least 70 percent of the variance in team engagement is explained by the quality of the manager or team leader."[13] How does a leader do it? Through a strong belief in the shared values and behaviors that constitute the core of the organization's culture and his or her ability to translate them into effective leadership.

We'll give leadership its due in chapter 8. The intent here is to concentrate on those decisions by leaders that create extraordinary places to work. It starts with mission, culture, and the team—why the organization exists in the first place and how it functions.

ENSURE EMPLOYEE IDENTIFICATION WITH THE MISSION, CULTURE, AND THE TEAM

Some organizations attract and retain employees by their very nature—airlines, purveyors of fashion merchandise, and firefighting, for example. They contribute to positive employee perceptions of the job. Others rely primarily on mission, culture, and the team to attract talent. The mission provides the "why" of the business. A culture often supported by a team-based organization reinforces the "how."

ADOPT AN EXPANDED VIEW OF CULTURE

For years, culture has been defined by academics in terms of several components: *shared assumptions* about such things as how an organization should work and what motivates people, *shared values* that suggest why members of an organization behave the way they do, *a set of accepted behaviors* that describe "how and why we do things around here," and certain *artifacts and customs* that have come to characterize an organization, such as preferred dress on the job or the annual company picnic.[14] These core elements of a culture are shown in bold print in box 2.1.

Changing any one of the elements of culture shown in box 2.1 becomes more difficult as one moves from artifacts and customs to shared assumptions and values. For example, it is a lot easier to alter the dress code (an artifact) than it is to identify and validate a needed change in shared values (such as a change from a physician-centered to a patient-centered focus in a hospital).

BOX 2.1: Core and related elements of culture*

- The organization's mission: What we hope to achieve.
- **Shared assumptions about people and the business: Why people want to work and why they come to our workplace.**
- **Values shared by organization members: What governs how and why we do what we do.**
- **Generally accepted behaviors: How and why we do things around here.**
- **Artifacts (customs and traditions): Things that identify us from others.**
- Measures of behaviors: What's going right and wrong.
- Actions triggered by the measures: How we recognize and correct behaviors.

*Items in bold print are generally regarded as core elements of culture

---

All of this takes place under the umbrella of the organization's mission. An inspirational mission can help attract talent, motivate people in their daily work, and provide goals that define long-term success. While not generally regarded as an element of culture, the mission provides the rationale for what an organization does, "why we do the things we do."

Leaders may concentrate on getting the shared values right. But if there is little emphasis on identifying and enforcing the behaviors that go with the values, *practically any set of values will do.* Don't even waste time trying to identify the values (or reshaping the culture). The effort will only create expectations within the organization that can't be met, with consequences that will only adversely affect performance.

Organizational culture typically is defined by the elements in bold print in box 2.1. That's alright if culture is regarded as a *thing.* But if it is to be employed in practice, a culture's core components have to be supplemented with measures and actions. Executives too often fall into the trap of establishing and communicating values and behaviors throughout an organization with little effort to follow up. As a result, employees may feel little ownership of the culture and that the shared values and behaviors are just an expression of what top management would like to see happening, not a description of how things work. This has given culture a bad name—one associated with the soft side of management. It helps explain why so many efforts to shape and sustain a culture are failures. The antidote is measurement and action.

INTEGRATE MISSION, CULTURE, AND STRATEGY

In the past, too many organizations have had as their missions, "to be the best (tire manufacturer, trucking company, etc.) in the world." That kind of mission might provide some inspiration to top executives but very little for employees down in the ranks. With the arrival of new generations of entrepreneurs with imaginations fueled by the internet and a need to compete for the best talent, mission statements have become inspirational in ways that we couldn't have imagined twenty-five years ago and in ways that younger employees have come to expect.

Google's mission to "organize and make available the world's information" is not a batch of empty words. Its efforts to do just that have inspired and attracted people with outstanding talent to the organization. At Airbnb, the room-sharing internet platform, the mission is "to create a more connected world." The company's culture, which has helped create a "best place to work," reflects that.[15]

These companies make an effort to integrate their missions with their cultures and strategies. Perhaps nowhere is this more true than at Salesforce, a provider of customer relationship management software-based solutions. Its vision is, in part, "We believe that the business of business is to improve the state of the world."[16] It has instituted policies for community involvement that demonstrate what that means. They include setting aside 1 percent of the company's equity and 1 percent of the company's product (with its employees often volunteering to install it) to support organizations dedicated to improving their communities. Additional funds support employee volunteer efforts. How does this fit with strategy? Even though Salesforce is not the highest-paying tech company in the San Francisco Bay Area, it can recruit the best of the talent it needs to succeed in delivering cloud-based customer relationship management services. Its support of active (vs. passive) philanthropy is an appeal that differentiates Salesforce from its competitors in one of the world's most competitive talent markets, San Francisco.

Inspirational missions, nontraditional cultures, and innovative strategies don't have to be confined to Silicon Valley or glamorous industries. Consider the savings bank industry, at one time dominated by uninspired leadership that wasn't very successful at getting Americans to save. I encountered it as a member of the North American Board of Dutch-based ING, a diverse financial services provider. The board was sitting through what we expected to be our last presentation of the day, one last dry recounting of numbers.

Instead, what we witnessed made an online savings bank, ING Direct, sound like the most exciting financial organization in the world. CEO Arkadi Kuhlmann, looking and sounding nothing like a banker (even though he had changed from his Harley-Davidson leather jacket to a business suit), told us not just how he was going to encourage savings but how his organization was going to "lead Americans back to saving." A cornerstone of the effort was the Orange (a nod to the Dutch) Code. Kuhlmann described it as a "constitution" comprising twelve "principles" intended to keep the organization from becoming "generic, cynical, and disengaged." Among the principles were "we will constantly learn, change, adapt, listen, invent, simplify, and dwell only in the present and the future. . . . We will never stop asking why or why not. . . . We will never be finished."[17]

The strategy Kuhlmann outlined included norm-bursting interest rates on savings up to eight times those of miserly (his term) competing traditional banks (easily affordable with interest rates at nearly all-time lows) and charges on loans a fraction of those charged by evil (again his term) credit card organizations, several of them located a stone's throw from ING Direct's U.S. headquarters in Wilmington, Delaware. It would continue to do it by hiring innovative people from outside the financial services industry who would go on to devise new forms of mortgages and other financial products. It would pioneer café banking—opening cafes with public, high-speed Wi-Fi connections (when there were few) where actual customers could manage their accounts and potential customers could establish them. This was how ING Direct was going to continue to be the fastest-growing bank in America. When Kuhlmann was finished, he had the board charged up and ready to go. The board's support did not go unrewarded. Less than ten years later, ING Direct, a company founded with very few resources, was sold to Capital One for $6.3 billion in cash and nearly 10 percent of Capital One's stock. And the café banks remain open today. The savings bank industry has never been the same. Inspirational missions, supportive nontraditional cultures, and accompanying innovative strategies foster good places to work in all kinds of industries.

RESULTS

Of course, none of this makes much sense if good places to work don't produce the best results. Here the evidence is quite clear. The matter has been well studied. As a result, we can conclude that employees registering high levels of employee engagement are more than twice as likely to remain on the job as those characterized as disengaged. They are more likely to refer friends and family members for employment. These factors lead to lower costs of recruitment, hiring, training, and lost productivity. U.S. companies spend almost $300 billion annually on recruiting and hiring new talent.[18] Employee engagement can be a significant contributor to the bottom line through retention alone. But that's not all.

We've noted that engaged employees are much more productive than the disengaged.[19] They are more loyal, less likely to be absent, work more safely on the job, produce fewer quality defects, and are less likely to steal. One estimate of the cost of active employee disengagement is that it costs U.S. employers $450 to $550 billion per year.[20]

Engaged employees foster higher levels of customer engagement that lead to higher customer loyalty, greater growth, and more profit. A Glassdoor study cited in chapter 3 links employee and customer satisfaction. Other studies have estimated the impact of customer satisfaction on profit and market value. For example, Claes Fornell and his colleagues compared data from the American Customer Satisfaction Index (ACSI) to company financial reports. They found, based on back-testing of stock portfolios, that "a firm's satisfied customers are likely to improve both the level and the stability of net cash flows. . . . In other words, it is possible to beat the market consistently by investing in firms that do well on the ACSI."[21]

This should not surprise us. Remember the results of a study of samples of great places to work cited in chapter 1? Researchers have concluded such workplaces produce significantly higher returns to investors than competitors not recognized as great places to work.[22]

In a nutshell, the Google, Airbnb, Salesforce, and ING Direct stories start with good leadership, an inspiring mission, attractive jobs, a great team, and an effective culture. This has enabled them to execute one or more strategies with success. It suggests several questions that we'll address in the next chapter: How important is an organization's culture in producing these results? How much does it contribute to the bottom line? Just how does this happen?

IF YOU REMEMBER NOTHING ELSE . . .

- Engaged employees are emotionally invested in and focused on creating value for their organizations every day. They are identified, among other things, by their willingness (at times) to put the organization's interests before their own, their willingness to refer friends and acquaintances (often with similar values and behaviors) as potential fellow employees, and their intent to remain with the organization.
- Important factors influencing the level of engagement in an organization are good leadership, an inspiring mission, attractive jobs, a great team, and an effective culture.

- The core of an organization's culture comprises: (1) shared assumptions about why people work, (2) shared values, (3) a common understanding about "how and why things are done around here," and (4) artifacts such as dress and other customs. It complements an organization's mission. But it relies on measurement and appropriate action when individuals stray from agreed-upon values and behaviors.
- Organizations generally do a very poor job of engaging employees; think of this as a competitive opportunity for those who do.

Chapter Three

HOW CULTURE DRIVES PERFORMANCE

FOLLOW THE MONEY

VAGUE BELIEFS about the importance of culture in competitive success apparently aren't enough to call into action the 76 percent of senior executives cited earlier who believe their organizations' performances could be improved by changes in culture but are doing little or nothing about it.[1]

This chapter is intended as a call to action. Words whisper. Numbers shout. Typically, organizational culture has been characterized by words, words with a soft edge. Not here. The objective here is to explore the impact of culture on sales and profit—namely, by the numbers. It's not something that needs to be done over and over. In fact, one time may be enough to convince employees from every division, department, and function of the organization just how importantly culture contributes to their success as well as the success of the organization.

Productivity is higher in organizations with effective cultures, of benefit to operations. Sales are higher in organizations with effective cultures, a matter of interest to the marketing people.

Innovation is higher as well, something that engineering and product development people will value. Employee morale and engagement numbers excel, making it easier for the human resources group to staff and retain talented employees. The resulting performance from all of this will put smiles on the faces of those responsible for financial outcomes. These effects contribute to the success of top management, at the same time making change of all kinds—including changes in strategy—easier.

This chapter is not just an academic exercise. The purpose here is to show that the impact of culture on operating profit can be measured, to show that it's possible. Along the way, it illustrates the potential economic impact of culture on every member of the organization. But most important of all, establishing the importance of culture to the organization provides an incentive to do whatever is necessary to shape a world-class culture out of whatever exists today in your organization. And to do it now with a high priority. It's time to follow the money.

To follow the money, I elicited the help of a subsidiary of a U.S.-based global professional services firm. A company that we'll call MarketCo, an operator of many branches with similar businesses, agreed to help. MarketCo executives provided both data and assistance in validating assumptions necessary to estimate the impact of culture on operating income. To do it, I compared data for pairs of branches. The objectives were just two: (1) predict the one with higher operating income (before that piece of information was disclosed to me), and (2) estimate how much of the difference in operating income was due to culture. Actual data from one pair of offices (that we'll name Chicago and Los Angeles) out of the several pairs for which I collected two years' worth of operating data is presented here to illustrate the process and the results. I selected two years to even out short-term fluctuations in the data.

The project required that we begin by identifying what I like to think of as pathways to performance and profit.

PATHWAYS TO PERFORMANCE AND PROFIT: THE "FIVE RS"

There are several important pathways connecting culture to productivity, growth, and profit. They can be measured with available organization data and a few assumptions. The results they produce are often surprising to CEOs. While survey research has shown that CEOs generally feel that culture is linked to financial performance, they often don't have a clear idea of just how this happens. And they often underestimate the impact.

In a nutshell, these pathways can be represented by five Rs: referrals from employees, retention of employees, returns to labor, referrals from customers, and relationships with customers. Let's follow these pathways for two of MarketCo's offices, Chicago and Los Angeles.

THE FIRST R: REFERRALS FROM EMPLOYEES

Engaged employees are generally thought to be more inclined to recommend family and friends as potential employees than those who are not so engaged.[2] Because employees are likely to recommend those who share the same attitude toward work as they do, an effort to hire referrals from the organization's best employees raises the quality of recruits while lowering costs of recruitment and selection. This also has a favorable impact on productivity that is measured later.

Successful referrals affect profit through this pathway:

More effective culture → Higher employee engagement → More employee referrals → Lower costs of recruitment → Higher profit

Referrals from employees are worth a lot. One estimate of recruiting, hiring, and training costs based on a meta-analysis of eleven research papers is that they represent from 10 to 30 percent of annual compensation for frontline employees up to more than 200 percent of annual compensation for those with higher-paid management skills.[3] This includes allowances for losses of productivity or sales as a result of employee turnover. Referrals reduce a portion of the costs associated with recruitment.

Computations of the impact of savings from referrals on operating profit for the Chicago and Los Angeles branches of MarketCo are shown in table 3.1. They are the result of (1) data supplied by the company, including the results of an employee engagement survey that was taken during the period under study; and (2) assumptions based on data from research as well as MarketCo management estimates.

A quick walk through the weeds of table 3.1: Start with the number of new hires referred by employees (from company records), sixteen for Chicago and three for Los Angeles. Multiply it by the annual compensation per employee for each branch—this gives us $1,842,360 for Chicago and $323,160 for Los Angeles. Assume some portion of this number is attributable to recruitment costs, all

TABLE 3.1 Two-year savings through referrals from employees, Chicago and Los Angeles branches of MarketCo*

	Chicago	Los Angeles
Employee engagement index (EEI)	3.93	4.17
Employee engagement index comparison	100.0%	106.1%
Number of new hires referred by employees	16	3
Average total annual compensation per employee	$109,180	$107,720
Total cost of recruitment, selection, and training (average for employees ranging from .41 of annual compensation for frontline employees to 2.41 of annual compensation for middle managers and above)	*x 1.0*	*x 1.0*
Share of cost represented by recruitment	*x .25*	*x .25*
Savings from referrals	$460,590	$85,850
Share of savings attributed to culture, adjusted for EEI†	*.50*	*.53*
Savings attributed to culture	$230,300	$45,500
Savings/revenue = percentage point increase in operating profit	.51	.25
Advantage in operating profit (in % points)	.26	

*Items in regular type represent actual data. Items in italics represent the author's assumptions.

†Chicago's assumed EEI was used as a base of .50; it was adjusted upward by 6% to recognize a higher EEI for Los Angeles.

of which are eliminated—in this case, I assumed ¼ of the total. Assume the share of these savings in recruitment costs attributed to culture, as reflected by results of the employee engagement index (50 percent for Chicago and 50 percent adjusted for higher engagement figures for Los Angeles, or 53 percent). Divide the resulting dollar savings attributed to culture in each case by two years of revenue for each branch.

As shown in table 3.1, savings from employee referrals due to organization culture represented .51 percentage points of operating profit for Chicago and .25 percentage points of operating profit for Los Angeles. In other words, Chicago's culture contributed .26 percentage points more to operating profit from employee referrals than Los Angeles' during the time under study. Even allowing for the fact that Chicago is a substantially larger office, it appeared to attract a proportionately larger number of referrals through its employees, an encouraging sign of an effective culture. But let's not jump to conclusions yet.

THE SECOND R: RETENTION OF EMPLOYEES

Loyal employees not only pass on knowledge of "how and why we do things around here," but they also reduce the need for replacing employees with its attendant recruiting, hiring, and training costs, thereby increasing profit.

Repeated studies have shown that highly engaged employees are more than twice as likely to remain on the job as those characterized as "disengaged."[4] This can produce significant reductions in the employee defection rate.

The pathway to profit associated with employee retention is as follows:

More effective culture → Higher employee engagement → Higher employee loyalty → Lower costs of recruitment and training → Higher profit

Data for the Chicago and Los Angeles branches of MarketCo produced the estimates calculated in table 3.2.

A quick walk through the weeds of table 3.2: We start with the number of voluntary and involuntary employee departures from the records of the Chicago and Los Angeles branches. Why the distinction? Because it's assumed that involuntary departures represent lower losses than voluntary departures. Those choosing to leave of their own accord are more likely to have better performance than those employees who are asked to leave. In this case, I assumed that an employee leaving voluntary cost a full year of compensation to replace while an employee leaving involuntarily cost half of that. This produced a total cost of replacing departed employees for the two years at $5,186,050 for Chicago and $1,293,040 for Los Angeles. Again, I assumed that about 50 percent of the cost of employee departures could be attributed to culture, as evidenced by the employee engagement index (EEI) adjusted to reflect a higher EEI for Los Angeles than for Chicago. I then divided the resulting costs by the revenues produced in each branch over the two years to get the relative costs of replacing departing employees as a percentage of revenue in each case.

Here we see that Chicago had a much higher defection rate for employees leaving the organization both voluntarily

TABLE 3.2 Two-year costs of replacing employees as a percentage of revenues (and operating profit), Chicago and Los Angeles branches of MarketCo*

	Chicago	Los Angeles
Employee engagement index (EEI)	3.93	4.17
Employee engagement index comparison	100.0%	106.1%
Employees departing voluntarily	43	10
One year's average compensation	$109,180	$107,720
Cost of a voluntary departure x average compensation	*x 1.0*	*x 1.0*
Total cost of voluntary departures	$4,694,740	$1,077,200
Employees departing involuntarily	8	4
Cost of an involuntary departure x average compensation	*.5*	*.5*
Total cost of involuntary departures	$436,720	$215,840
Total cost of employee departures	$5,186,050	$1,293,040
Share of cost attributed to culture, adjusted for difference in EEI	*.53*	*.5*
Cost of employee departures attributed to culture	$2,748,610	$646,520
Two-year revenue	$45.1 million	$17.8 million
Cost of departures due to culture as % of revenue	6.09%	3.63%
Operating profit advantage (in percentage points)	2.46	

*Items in regular type represent actual data. Items in italics represent the author's assumptions.

and involuntarily. Assuming 1.0 times an employee's annual salary to estimate the costs of an employee's voluntary departure and .5 times an employee's annual salary for the costs of an involuntary departure, we see that a much higher rate of both voluntary and involuntary employee defections at the Chicago branch produces high replacement costs, resulting in costs compared to revenues that are 2.46 percentage points higher for Chicago than for Los Angeles. With this added information, it now appears that one reason the Los Angeles branch had a lower rate of employee referrals, as we noted earlier, was that it needed to replace fewer employees in the first place.

THE THIRD R: RETURNS TO LABOR (PRODUCTIVITY)

Not only are engaged employees more loyal than the disengaged, but they are also more productive—in service industries, 21 percent more productive than the disengaged, according to one study.[5] Members of the Gallup organization also estimate that teams with high employee engagement rates are 21 percent more productive than those with low engagement rates. They go on to say that this translates into "18 percent higher revenue per employee compared with the average."[6] It results not only in lower labor costs per unit of revenue but also higher profit. It is at the heart of this pathway to profit:

More effective culture → Higher employee engagement → Higher employee loyalty → Higher productivity → Lower labor cost per unit of revenue → Higher profit

Productivity comparisons, measured in labor costs to revenues, for the Chicago and Los Angeles branches of MarketCo are shown in table 3.3.

A quick walk through the weeds of table 3.3: This one is simple. I compared the total labor costs of the two branches as a proportion of their respective two-year revenues and assumed that half of the difference in percentages was due to culture.

The productivity comparisons indicate that labor costs in relation to revenues—a rough indicator of productivity—are lower in Los Angeles than in Chicago. This could be due to many factors, such as greater use of technology at one site than another (not a factor here) or lower wage or pricing structures in one city as opposed to another. The studies cited above suggest that differences in an organization's culture, reflected in employee engagement, are also a major influence on productivity.

TABLE 3.3 Two-year differences in productivity contributions to operating profit, Chicago and Los Angeles branches of MarketCo*

	Chicago	Los Angeles
Labor costs as a proportion of revenues	47.5%	46.1%
Differential favoring low-cost branch (in percentage points)		1.4%
Proportion of differential attributed to culture		50%
Differential credited to Los Angeles branch (in percentage points)		.70

*Items in regular type represent actual data. Items in italics represent the author's assumptions.

If half of the difference in productivity is attributed to culture, it suggests that culture contributed .70 percentage points more to operating profit in Los Angeles vs. Chicago, as shown in table 3.3.

There is one caveat in trying to estimate differences in productivity. Small changes in productivity rarely have an immediate effect on labor costs because they may not add up to the output of an individual employee. Thus, employment may be sticky in the face of productivity increases up to the point where a full day's work can be eliminated. For example, a one percentage point increase in productivity might result in one less job only in workplaces employing one hundred or more people. Over the long term and in larger organizations, however, this pathway can produce profit differences.

THE FOURTH R: RELATIONSHIPS WITH CUSTOMERS (REFERRALS)

Engaged employees communicate their enthusiasm to customers, positively affecting customer engagement as well. Repeated studies have shown this relationship, one my colleagues and I have referred to as a mirror effect, to be common in many organizations.[7] One recent study of 293 companies across 13 industries by Glassdoor, a website that lets workers assess employers, linked its data to a measure of shoppers' sentiment, the American Customer Satisfaction Index. It found significant relationships between employee and customer satisfaction, especially in industries where "workers have the most direct contact with customers."[8]

Currently engaged customers are important sources of referrals of new customers. This is important because the biggest culture-related impact a customer can have on profit is from word of mouth. This pathway to profit is:

More effective culture → Higher employee engagement → Higher customer engagement → More customer referrals → Lower selling costs per unit of revenue → Higher profit and faster growth

Research has shown that the best customers, in terms of sales volume, are the best sources of new customer referrals.[9] Not only are such referrals effective, but they also lead to even higher levels of engagement among those providing the references. Organizations that rely on their best customers for new business referrals thus make a good customer even more profitable through the lifetime stream of profit generated from new business. This helps explain, for example, why companies like Intuit, the personal financial software provider, have so few salespeople. Intuit relies heavily on favorable word-of-mouth from its best customers.

Unfortunately, too many organizations don't track revenue obtained from customer referrals even though it is not difficult to collect. This was the case at MarketCo. With the help of management, it required that I come up with an assumed rate of referred business for the two branches. Fortunately, I did have the results of employee engagement surveys for both branches for the two-year period. They provided composite scores (on a seven-point scale) for employee engagement of 3.93 for Chicago and 4.17 for Los Angeles. Assuming employee engagement translates directly into customer referrals, I assumed a comparably higher referral rate on new business for Los Angeles, with the computations shown in table 3.4.

A quick walk through the weeds of table 3.4: Here I started with the number of clients new to the Chicago and Los Angeles branches in each of two years. All were assumed to arrive in the middle of each year. Thus, those arriving in the first year produced a year and a half of sales; those arriving in the second produced half a year of sales. Using these assumptions, I estimated years of sales from new clients for both branches. I then multiplied this by a factor of 40 percent, representing the proportion of new sales from client referrals attributed to relations with engaged employees, estimated by management for Chicago. A higher proportion, 42.4 percent, was again used for Los Angeles to reflect its higher employee engagement index. This produced an estimate of years of new client sales due to culture. Multiplying these numbers by the average annual revenues for all clients for the two branches produced a new revenue estimate. Next, I had to assume operating profit earned on the new business. Although management knew this number, according to the terms of my agreement with MarketCo it was not to be disclosed to me until my estimates were completed. So I had to assume the target operating profit number set for many of the company's branches operating under normal conditions, 15 percent. Applying this proportion produced a number for operating profit from new business which, when compared with two-year revenues for the two branches, yielded estimates of percentage points of operating profit on revenue.

As a result of the data presented in table 3.4, I estimated that during the two years under examination, the Los Angeles

TABLE 3.4 Estimate of operating profit generated as a result of customer referrals due to differences in culture, as a share of total revenue, two-year period, Chicago and Los Angeles branches of MarketCo*

	Chicago	Los Angeles
Employee engagement index (EEI)	3.93	4.17
EEI comparison	100.0%	106.1%
New clients	12	10
Years of sales to new clients (over two-year period)†	*11*	*8*
Proportion of new clients referred due to employee engagement††	40%	42.4%
Years of new client sales due to employee engagement	4.4	3.4
Average annual revenue per client	$601,250	$331,920
Revenue from client referrals due to employee engagement	$2,646,600	$1,129,000
Assumed operating profit on revenue	*15%*	*15%*
Operating profit from client referrals due to employee engagement	$397,000	$169,000
Total two-year revenue	$45.1 million	$17.8 million
Percentage points of operating profit on revenue from client referrals due to employee engagement	.88	.95
Differential advantage to Los Angeles branch (in % points)		.07

*Items in regular type represent actual data. Items in italics represent the author's assumptions.

†New clients referred in the first year × 1.5 years + new clients referred in the second year × .5 = years of sales from new clients.

††MarketCo could not provide data on new business gained from referrals by current clients. Therefore, the proportion of new clients referred due to employee engagement for Chicago was assumed based on rough estimates by management. The proportion for Los Angeles was then increased by the increment of EEI achieved by the Los Angeles branch.

branch earned a slight increment over Chicago from customer referrals, .07 percentage points of operating profit on revenue, as shown in table 3.4.

THE FIFTH R: RELATIONSHIPS WITH CUSTOMERS (RETENTION AND DEFECTIONS)

This substantial source of growth and profit comes from fixing the leaky bucket of customer defections. Fewer lost customers reduce the need for new customer development to achieve a sales goal.

Too many organizations spend too much of their time and budget replacing lost sales with costly-to-develop new business, essentially churning their customer base. One classic study concluded that loyal customers buy more than new customers, are less costly to serve, and provide higher margins on sales over time.[10] From a loyal base, efforts to attract new customers provide a net addition to sales and profit. For this reason, customer defections have to be taken very seriously. Of course, some departures may be welcomed, especially by employees. These are the customers whose demands are nearly impossible to meet or those who demean and verbally abuse an organization's employees. The implicit assumption underlying the computations in table 3.5 is that all departing customers are of at least average attractiveness, in terms of sales volume, margins, and engaging relationships.

This is the pathway to profit:

More effective culture → Higher employee engagement → Higher customer engagement → Fewer customer defections → Lower selling costs per unit of revenue → Higher profit and faster growth

TABLE 3.5 Comparative effect of client loyalty (defections) on operating profit over two-year period, Chicago and Los Angeles branches of MarketCo*

	Chicago	Los Angeles
Employee engagement index (EEI)	3.93	4.17
EEI comparison	100.0%	106.1%
Client defections	39	22
Years of client revenue lost from midyear defections†	*43.5*	*24*
Proportion of defections due to employee engagement††	*26.5%*	*25%*
Years of client revenue lost due to employee engagement	*11.5*	*6.0*
Annual revenue per client	$601,250	$331,920
Revenue lost from client defections due to employee engagement	*$6,914,000*	*$1,991,000*
Goal for operating profit on revenue (all branches)	*15%*	*15%*
Operating profit lost from client defections due to employee engagement	$1,037,000	$298,000
Total two-year revenue	$45.1 million	$17.8 million
Percentage points of lost operating profit/ revenue	2.30	1.67
Operating profit advantage		.63

*Items in regular type represent actual data. Items in italics represent the author's assumptions.

†Client defections in the first year × 1.5 years + client defections in the second year × .5 years = total years of revenue lost due to client defections.

††At the moment of this computation, relative rates of operating profit on revenue were not known to the author. Therefore, a target rate of 15% used by MarketCo in its profit planning for many of its branches was assumed.

The same mirror effect described above in connection with customer referrals of new business applies here as well. Employee loyalty, expressed in terms of the engagement index, influences customer loyalty, as shown in the computations in table 3.5.

A quick walk through the weeds of table 3.5: This is a mirror image of the calculations in table 3.4. In this case, we're estimating revenue losses from clients who've defected rather than revenue gains from new business. Management provided records of the number of clients defecting in each of two years. Assuming all defections were midyear (since actual dates were not available), I estimated losses of 1.5 years of revenue for first-year defections and .5 years of revenue for second-year defections. Multiplying years and numbers of defections produced a figure for years of revenue lost for all client defections, 43.5 in the case of Chicago, 24 for Los Angeles. Next, I assumed the proportion of departures due to culture (lack of employee engagement). Here, I used a base of one client out of four for Los Angeles and a slightly higher figure for Chicago to reflect a lower employee engagement index for that branch. This gave me years of revenue loss due to culture which, when multiplied by average client revenues per year for each branch, provided a number for the revenue lost by each branch—$6,914,000 for Chicago and $1,991,000 for Los Angeles. An assumed operating profit of 15 percent (for which management, by agreement, withheld information until I had concluded the relative profitability of the Chicago and Los Angeles branches) on the revenue was again employed to arrive at a number for losses in operating profit for each branch. This could then be compared to revenues to create *relative estimates of operating profit losses in percentage points of revenue.*

Applying several assumptions noted above, the most important of which had to do with margins on the business, we see that the Los Angeles branch enjoyed an advantage of .63 percentage points of operating profit on revenue over Chicago.

Putting the results of these computations together, as shown in table 3.6, we see that factors associated with culture were estimated to give Los Angeles a 3.60 percentage point operating profit advantage over Chicago. As I did with other pairs of MarketCo branches, I delivered my expectation to management that the Los Angeles branch would be the most profitable. Then the curtain was pulled back to disclose actual profit figures.

TABLE 3.6 Percentage point comparisons of operating profit performance of the Chicago and Los Angeles branches of MarketCo on the five pathways to profit

	Advantage to:	
	Chicago	Los Angeles
Pathway one: referrals from employees	.26	
Pathway two: retention of employees		2.46
Pathway three: returns to labor (productivity)		.70
Pathway four: referrals from customers		.07
Pathway five: retention/defections of customers		.63
Totals	.26	3.86
Differential		3.60

WHAT HAPPENED WHEN MANAGEMENT
PULLED BACK THE CURTAIN?

As a result of my estimates of the impact of culture on operating profit at MarketCo's Chicago and Los Angeles branches, I concluded that the Los Angeles branch operating profit advantages through culture for Los Angeles vs. Chicago added up to 3.60 percentage points, money that should drop to the bottom line in the form of greater operating income. The question in my mind when management gave me actual financial results was not whether the Los Angeles branch would turn out to be more profitable than the Chicago branch. The question was, by how much?

At this point in our study, MarketCo's management disclosed actual results for its various branches. They showed that during the two years in question, annualized operating profit on revenue at Los Angeles was 22.5 percentage points, 9.15 percentage points higher than at Chicago. Bingo! Further, when comparing my estimates of the effect of culture on this number, I could estimate that *culture contributed 39.3 percent (3.60/9.15) of that difference.* These are admittedly rough calculations, but they are directionally correct.

In my study, I compared other pairs of MarketCo's branches as well. My predictions of relative financial performance, using largely nonfinancial data, were all directionally correct. The impact of culture on differentials in operating income as percentages of revenue was substantial in every case.

By now you're asking yourself how I know that the assumptions shown in italics in the tables are correct. I don't. They are based on data from various studies, but your number may be just as good as mine. Plug in your estimates and go through the exercise. Your result will be different. But I predict that it will impress you as much as my result impressed me. The degree to which culture influences operating profit, based on your data and assumptions, will be remarkable.

Estimates such as these will vary from one organization to another. The highest estimates of the impact of culture on operating income will be highest for those organizations with the highest proportion of employees engaged in face-to-face contact with customers, such as in performing the services offered by the example company, MarketCo. But the numbers shown here are probably not surprising to leaders of organizations that have achieved competitive success through their cultures as well as their strategies.

WHAT'S THIS ESTIMATE GOOD FOR?

Why estimate the impact of culture on operating profits? The purpose is to motivate efforts to reshape an existing culture. Usually, it's only necessary to do it once to motivate top management to begin the process. The idea is to start the culture change process backed up with numbers, not just with heartfelt but vague beliefs.

WHAT ABOUT INNOVATION?

I've left out of my estimates an important source of profit: innovation. In part, it is a function of the stream of suggestions for product and service improvements put forth by employees and customers. Limited evidence suggests that engaged employees and customers are more likely to recommend product and service improvements than those who are not engaged. One study my colleagues and I carried out at Caesar's Entertainment supports this notion. In it, we surveyed data for over four thousand members of the company's Total Rewards customer loyalty program.

Caesar's uses a unique system for identifying the value of customer loyalty. Based on early purchase patterns, it estimates lifetime value that they will generate for the company. They range from gold ($2,000 lifetime value) to seven star ($50,000 in value per year). We inquired about the frequency with which each category of customer recommended product or service improvements, not being sure what we would find. After all, while seven star customers would seem to be more engaged, given the level of their gaming activity, we assumed that they also might be more affluent, busier, and less likely to spend time with suggestions for improvement. We were wrong.

To our surprise, we found that seven star customers offered more than twice as many suggestions for product and service improvements as did gold customers. Further, they were 16 percent more willing than gold customers to attend a gathering organized by Caesar's (Harrah's at the time) to identify new service ideas.[11]

Other evidence suggests that higher rates of innovation are also associated with organizations in which collaboration, transparency, and low or nonexistent organizational boundaries are valued and taken advantage of.[12] All of these result from the shared values and behaviors at a culture's core.

CULTURE, EMPLOYEE ENGAGEMENT, AND PROFIT

The pathways to performance and profit make up a culture profit model shown in figure 3.1. Combined with calculations shown in the tables, it provides a roadmap that can be followed by any organization in estimating the impact of culture on its profits. It's important to note a couple of things about the model.

EMPLOYEE ENGAGEMENT IS CENTRAL

Note that each of the pathways relies on employee engagement. The impact of employee engagement on employee loyalty, productivity, and ownership (referrals and suggestions for new products and processes) as well as on customer engagement, loyalty, and ownership is substantial. As we saw earlier, employees registering high (vs. average or low) levels of engagement are more likely to remain on the job, more likely to refer friends and family members for employment, more likely to be more productive, and more likely to enhance customer engagement in those industries in which customer face time is important.

AND THAT'S NOT ALL

The primary pathways to profit from an effective culture don't even include the full effect of some other sources of growth and profit from employee engagement. Highly engaged employees are less likely to be absent, to work more safely on the job, and to produce fewer quality defects. They are even less likely to steal.[13] Some of these behaviors show up in terms of improved

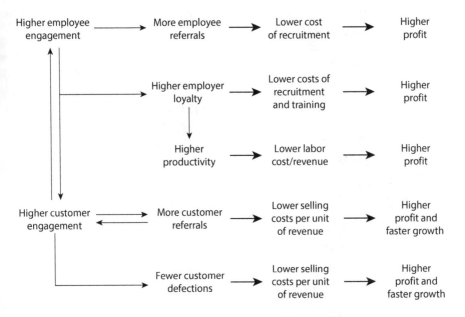

FIGURE 3.1 Culture profit model

Source: Adapted from James L. Heskett, *The Culture Cycle: How to Shape the Unseen Force That Transforms Performance* (Englewood Cliffs, NJ: Pearson, 2012), 115.

productivity. But all of the behaviors are associated with higher customer loyalty, greater growth, and more profit.

Given all this, it should be no surprise that numerous studies have—without measuring intermediate relationships or pathways described above—established strong correlations between employee engagement and business outcomes. In one of the most extensive meta-analyses of 42 studies covering 198,000 respondents in 36 independent companies, one team of researchers concluded that "business units above the median on employee engagement had a 70 percent . . . higher success rate (on composite business-unit performance) than those below the median on employee engagement."[14]

WHERE DOES STRATEGY FIT?

Over the years I've asked many senior executives the following question: Which organization is going to perform better, one with a good strategy and poor execution or one with a mediocre strategy and good execution? Those that favor a good strategy typically give less weight to the importance of culture than those that favor good execution.

Include me in the group favoring execution. Larry Bossidy, a successful CEO, and Ram Charan, a senior consultant, have made a persuasive argument for this point of view. As they put it: "An astonishing number of strategies fail because leaders don't make a realistic assessment of whether the organization can execute the plan."[15]

Don't get me wrong. A good strategy is a critical element of an organization's performance. It has its own pathways to profit that are not our major concern here. It can support an organization until a competitor with a better strategy comes along. But it produces less enduring competitive advantage than an organization's culture, primarily because it is more visible and therefore more subject to reverse engineering by competitors.

Strategy has less influence on employee engagement than culture. And employee engagement is, after all, at the heart of the culture profit model.

Knowing what we've just discussed, wouldn't you suppose that employee engagement should be at or near the top of the list of priorities for management? If it is, managers around the world are failing badly on this priority, as we will see all too dramatically in the next chapter. That's why it's so important to understand why some organizations engage both employees and customers better than others. It's our next concern.

IF YOU REMEMBER NOTHING ELSE . . .

- The relative profitability of two organizations in the same business can be predicted with a high degree of accuracy utilizing only culture-related information.
- Data from your organization, when combined with external data and estimates, can be used to estimate the impact of culture on profit.
- The resulting estimate of the impact of culture on profit can provide an important motivator to change a culture.
- Pathways to profit from culture all lead through employee engagement.
- It requires less leadership time and cost to foster and lead a high-engagement culture than it does to foster and lead a low-engagement culture; returns from the former can be enormous.

Chapter Four

WHY SOME ORGANIZATIONS ENGAGE EMPLOYEES (AND CUSTOMERS) BETTER THAN OTHERS

AT FIRST glance, John Legere was a strange choice to head up a wireless carrier company. There couldn't have appeared to be a poorer fit between the person—characterized in the media as a rebel, a rock star, and a huge competitor—and a wireless industry dominated by AT&T and Verizon for years. But Legere knew what he was getting into when he agreed to become CEO of Deutsche Telekom's U.S.-based wireless communications carrier, T-Mobile, in 2012. With more than twenty years of experience in the industry, he had a notion that he could, out of the limited resources of a subsidiary of a foreign owner as well as an underdog player in an asset-intensive business, build a company that could shake up the industry. This wasn't so farfetched. The wireless industry was populated by customers locked into contracts for services that often didn't match their needs. It's one that Legere characterized as "stupid, broken, arrogant," one "hated" by its customers even though few could do without it.[1]

It was ripe for shaking up, and Legere sought to do it by creating a culture that aligned with a strategy built on breaking industry norms—no customer contracts, anytime upgrades, an international network—in short, the UNcarrier.

To change the culture, he needed young, enthusiastic frontline people to match a customer base that skewed young, twenty-eight or twenty-nine year olds. To attract and engage those people to an industry tired before its time, his team came up with an inspiring mission, "build the future of technology." They helped him and his leadership team put together values, accepted behaviors, and artifacts, including a distinctive company color (magenta) as well as paraphernalia to enable employees to become the living embodiment of the company's brand. This gave them the ammunition needed to execute the first big initiative built around the notion of hiring for attitude, training for skills.

HIRE FOR ATTITUDE, TRAIN FOR SKILLS

The challenge begins with hiring the right people, those who buy into an organization's mission, values, and behaviors ("how and why we do things around here"). Meeting this challenge not only enhances a place to work, it can save on the substantial costs of replacing departing employees later. Best of all, it reduces the costs of managing the mistakes, efforts that often end up in failure. Some people are more prone to become enthusiastic about a set of ideas and practices than others. Based on work with a number of organizations, I've found that the best follow a simple tenet: *Hire for attitude, train for skills.*

Under Legere, T-Mobile's leadership team sought to attract the kinds of employees that could relate to its young customer base. It did it, in part, through a set of values that included "(1) Customer delight drives our actions; (2) Go big—stay scrappy; (3) Respect and integrity guide our behavior; (4) I am T-Mobile—count on me; (5) Team together and (6) Best place to perform and grow."[2] That's the formal message. The informal message was a website that celebrated fun and success led by a CEO who set out to personify the company's brand and who called his larger competitors, AT&T and Verizon, "dumb and dumber."[3] Self-selection into the T-Mobile organization resulted in employees who related to its values. At the time, it was repeatedly in the top ranks of various employee polls as a great place to work, even in a "boring" industry.

Hiring for attitude works everywhere, even in medical organizations hiring doctors where, in the early days, I was nearly asked to leave meetings where I proposed it. It is particularly important, for example, in police work. It was a challenge faced by the New York Police Department some years ago as it transitioned to a strategy of community policing emphasizing involvement with the citizenry as a means of reducing crime. Tests showed that too many recruits were attracted to a job that enabled them to carry a gun and use it to exercise power over others. The selection process for entry into the police academy had to be altered to reflect the change in strategy. News stories about the use of unnecessary force remind us that it has taken years for the NYPD to fully staff its front line with officers who have the desired attitude in an organization that finds it very difficult to fire people.

The NYPD knows how to train for skills. Like nearly every organization I've studied, its leaders are amateurs when it comes to changing the values of people who, once hired, represent a bad fit with the organization and its culture. Such efforts are rarely successful and eat up large amounts of time and money. Richard Fairbanks, chairman and CEO of Capital One, put it best when he commented that, "At most companies, people spend 2 percent of their time recruiting and 75 percent managing their recruiting mistakes."[4]

How do you hire for attitude? It requires more than just asking about whether a prospective employee identifies with a mission and culture. More likely, we find out more when we pose situations involving at least two difficult choices that tell us how a prospect might perform under a specific set of circumstances. Or we can ask about the most important and difficult decisions that a candidate has had to make in the past and how they were resolved. The choice of the decision may be just as important as the way it was resolved in telling us about the candidate's attitude. In reading essays on admissions forms at Harvard Business School, we noted the choice of topics as well as the tendency to use the pronouns *we* or *I*.

A group interview typical of many that Southwest Airlines conducts (one of which I witnessed) illustrates how to hire for attitude. At Southwest, as many as fifty job candidates are seated in a large room. Among other things, each is asked to stand and describe the most embarrassing moment in their lives. (This generates some incredible stories, by the way.) There are red faces and a lot of laughter, some of it uneasy. Those doing the hiring, however, are not watching the person speaking. They are watching others in the group to find those who are empathizing with the speaker. It's those people who will best relate to Southwest's customers and other employees.[5]

Hiring for attitude takes time. So when Amazon announced, as it did in August 2017, that it planned to hire 50,000 people in one day into an organization with about 350,000 employees, what is the likelihood that a high proportion of those new hires ended up engaged?[6] Probably pretty low.

BUILD A GREAT WORKPLACE ON WHAT EMPLOYEES TELL US

We can assume what constitutes a great workplace. Or we can ask employees. When we do, the reasons most often cited are the quality of leadership ("my boss"); the opportunity for personal development; whether my work is recognized; the quality of my colleagues; delegation of authority—personal latitude, within limits and with accountability, to produce results; and reasonable pay, often in that order. All of these except pay are directly related to culture.[7]

This set of attributes determines the quality of a workplace. So it's useful to consider examples of just how it's achieved.

FOSTER TRUST THROUGH "NO-SURPRISES LEADERSHIP"

Trust is the bedrock for employee engagement. A culture that fosters trust reduces what academics call transactional "friction."

As a result, decisions are made and implemented faster and at lower cost, something critical in an age where speed takes on greater and greater value.[8] At a recent business conference, Brian Chesky, cofounder and CEO of Airbnb, commented, "Things move at the speed of trust."[9] It could hardly be more true than in a business like Airbnb, where a platform-based business bringing those with rooms and travelers together relies on a triangle of trust between the company, its landlords, and traveler-renters, all of whom operate to a great extent on a sight-unseen basis requiring a high level of trust.

When probed, employees describe good leaders in terms of whether or not they are fair. Digging deeper, fairness is judged on whether leaders hire, recognize, promote, and fire the right people. The leader is on trial, with peers and subordinates serving as members of her jury deciding whether they can trust her or not.

People like to know, for example, that their boss exercises good judgment in dealing with them and their colleagues. When there is agreement, there are no surprises. When employees are surprised by a personnel move by their boss, they ask why. If there isn't a good explanation, trust in their boss takes a hit.

Think of this as "no-surprises leadership" in which leaders try to avoid surprising their employees, as opposed to the long-held notion that it's the employees who are expected not to surprise their leaders. No-surprises leadership results from a leader's excellent communication, a certain amount of transparency, and even a willingness to risk psychological vulnerability (admitting errors or seeking and taking advice from others), all of which help build trust. This requires people who both lead and follow with a strong sense of the values, behaviors, measures, and actions that ensure that everyone is working from the same strong foundation based on shared assumptions—a basic element of culture. When information and decisions have to be kept confidential because of their critical nature, it requires that the reasons later are made clear to employees. Transparency is the rule, not the exception.

We can put some numbers on this. In a meta-analysis of several studies, Kurt Dirks and Donald Ferrin concluded that "trust in leadership positively affects employees' job performance, overall job satisfaction, and commitment to their organizations." One study of 6,500 Holiday Inn employees concluded that when they rated their trust in their manager on a five-point scale, a 1/8 point improvement in the average produced a 2.5 percent improvement in unit revenue or $250,000 in added revenue per hotel.[10]

ENSURE PSYCHOLOGICAL SAFETY

Great places to work demand a lot from their employees. They are characterized by a willingness to put the organization before other interests. At times, this involves grueling hours and high expectations. That's why it's so important to create what Amy Edmondson has termed a "fearless organization."[11]

Characteristics of a fearless organization include trust, psychological safety (the belief that the work environment is safe for interpersonal risk-taking) and voice (the freedom to speak out with some assurance of being heard) when the situation demands it. These are complementary workplace conditions that have been shown to contribute to high levels of worker engagement. They involve different leadership behaviors. On the one hand, trust requires predictability, a kind of vulnerability, and openness on the part of leaders. Psychological safety concerns itself with the elimination of the fear of speaking out, sharing ideas, and offering constructive criticism. Voice also requires a willingness to listen on the part of the leader.

Trust and psychological safety contribute to inclusiveness in the workplace, learning, and innovation. According to Edmondson, who has studied the phenomenon for many years, psychological safety reduces or eliminates the fear of expressing voice, allowing associates to feel free to contribute ideas, provide constructive criticism, examine their own and others' mistakes for lessons, and offer advice that is critical to an environment in which employees both learn and innovate. Studies have shown that fear inhibits learning and cooperation. It fosters an "epidemic of silence." More importantly, it is not a motivator, especially in the long run. This has taken on new meaning in an age when reporting and litigation of inappropriate workplace behavior is recognized as a critical element of a good workplace.

The absence of psychological safety often pervades authoritarian cultures. It can lead to outcomes experienced by Volkswagen, a story worth pausing a moment to consider in box 4.1. It's about a storied global organization in which leadership discouraged voice among engineers asked to develop software to avoid detection of diesel vehicle high pollution levels. Fear of management retaliation may well have kept them quiet when they should have been objecting. Psychological safety, combined with receptive leadership, might have saved the company

BOX 4.1: Consequences of insufficient psychological safety at Volkswagen?

Volkswagen is an engineer's home. Engineering is honored at Volkswagen to the same degree that design and designers reign at Apple. It is the path to the top. To work at Volkswagen is to have a career, not a job. It means that you are the center of attention at social gatherings in Wolfsberg, the company's German home. It is a badge of honor—or at least it was.

Volkswagen represents itself as being guided by three values: social responsibility (largely to employees and their communities), sustainability ("it means that we conduct our business activities on a responsible and long-term basis"), and a spirit of partnership ("good jobs and careful treatment of resources and the environment form the basis for generating lasting value").* Martin Winterkorn, former CEO, and Matthew Müller, his successor, either forgot those values or deliberately violated them if allegations against them prove to be true. It's alleged that they actively or tacitly approved work to design and produce diesel vehicles that violated pollution standards while deceiving regulators. At the time, Volkswagen was attempting to surpass Toyota as the world's largest automaker by promoting the concept of "clean diesel." The goal was ambitious, the prize was large.

This sad episode began with an innovative solution to a problem. It involved the development, during the time that Müller was head of project management at Audi in 2006, of a way to eliminate the clanking sound made by diesel vehicles when they were started. The solution increased pollution levels over established standards. If corrected to meet pollution standards, the solution would have added too much weight (in the form of stored chemicals) to the vehicle. One answer was to develop software that automatically turned off the noise reducer during emission testing. It was tempting, but it was illegal. The temptation was too attractive to top management, given the organization's lofty goal. How could such accomplished engineers, including Winterkorn and Müller, succumb to the temptation? And why did some of the world's best automotive engineers comply without raising their voices?

Engineers undoubtedly felt the pressure of a long-standing culture comprising equal parts of pride, arrogance, and fear. Since the company's founding by the designer of the Volkswagen Beetle, Ferdinand Porsche, employees had experienced what has been called authoritarian leadership. According to one commentary, the cheating was fueled by engineers "fearful of contradicting their superiors and . . . afraid to admit failure."[†] In other words, absence of psychological safety.

It may have resulted as well from a phenomenon, "normalization of deviance," commonly found in engineering-dominated organizations. It describes the process under which, little by little, standards are "stretched" and violated until they produce an unworkable or even illegal solution that doesn't feel like cheating. It's the same phenomenon, again possibly combined with a lack of psychological safety, attributed to the engineering work on the O-rings that led to the failure of the Challenger rocket.[††]

The knowledge that senior managers were either encouraging or condoning this practice had to have spread beyond the engineering departments at Audi and Volkswagen. One can imagine the shrugged shoulders and resigned attitudes as employees observed behaviors that ran counter to the companies' values. It was "not how things are usually done around here." In a sense, hard-to-measure organizational psychological damage was occurring. It was magnified when the practice was discovered in 2015 by regulators in the United States. The discovery led to immediate accusations in the German press that the United States was trying to damage a competitor of U.S. automakers. But ultimately it resulted in a personal apology to the U.S. president from Müller.

The measurable cost to Volkswagen is well known. It has pled guilty to violating laws in both the United States and Germany, reserved more than $30 billion for the payment of legal fines, recalled and repaired its products, and paid compensation to Volkswagen dealers who suffered a decline in the value of their franchises. But these are just the costs that can be easily measured.

One report of a suit filed against the company concludes that "the decision . . . was not . . . made by 'a couple of software engineers.' Rather, it was the result of a willful and systematic scheme of cheating by dozens of employees at all levels of the company."§ Among others, former CEOs Winterkorn and Müller have been indicted.

Imagine the blow to the pride of the vast majority of loyal and honest Volkswagen employees that this scandal represents. Picture the conversations involving Volkswagen employees at social functions in Wolfsburg now. What effect has this had on Volkswagen as a place to work or do business with? As an employee, whom and what do you trust? And if you see something, can you say something?

˙Volkswagen-karriere.de, accessed September 1, 2016.
†Jack Ewing and Graham Bowley, "The Engineering of Volkswagen's Aggressive Ambition," *New York Times*, December 13, 2015.
††See Diane Vaughn, *The Challenger Launch Decision: Risky Technology, Culture, and Deviance at NASA* (Chicago: University of Chicago Press, 1996).
§Jack Ewing and Hiroko Tabuchi, "Volkswagen Scandal Reaches All the Way to the Top, Lawsuits Say," *New York Times*, July 19, 2016.

from facing criminal charges, fines and penalties, and public embarrassment.

So how does one go about building psychological safety? Edmondson suggests, among other things, reframing failure primarily as an opportunity to learn, emphasizing why voice (elimination of fear to contribute) is important, reminding people of "why what they do matters," inviting others to participate by being a "don't knower" who practices "humble listening," purposeful probing to find out "what others are seeing," sincerely expressing appreciation for contributions by others, "destigmatizing failure," and, when necessary, sanctioning actions by members of the organization that increase rather than reduce fear.[12] Highly engaged employees want to know how they're doing. Leaders minimize the anxiety that these employees sometimes experience on the job by providing rapid evaluation and feedback.

DEVELOP PEOPLE THAT ATTRACT
OTHER GOOD PEOPLE

Winners like to work with winners. Losers also like to work with winners. But winners don't like to work with losers.

Studies of work have shown that engaged employees are up to 2.5 times more productive than the disengaged.[13] Given this, it should be no surprise that high producers want to work with other high producers. Or that low producers can drive high producers from an organization, thus beginning a race to the bottom, as measured in productivity.

Good places to work attract good employees in part because they appeal to people attracted by the same set of organizational values and behaviors. They value people and their development. And they provide latitude to produce results with a high degree of accountability and recognition for achievement. They are often demanding places to work, in part because people are devoted to success in jobs they value.

The proliferation of millennials—those reaching the age of twenty-one by the year 2000—in the workplace has influenced talent development practices. Millennials especially value personal development, constant feedback, and recognition, all of which far outweigh compensation (as long as it is reasonable) in their minds. At first, this earned millennials a bad reputation among many employers and their older bosses. But their energy and productivity have forced many leaders to give them the benefit of the doubt.

This has begun to trigger changes in training, coaching, and evaluation practices. For example, leaders harnessing the potential of millennials have found that frequent, immediate feedback as part of a process of learning and personal development works. The time-honored annual employee review process, at least the way it's typically practiced, doesn't work.

Now, of course, comes Gen Z, the generation following millennials into the workforce. They appear to be motivated differently, quite possibly as a result of coming of age during what became known as the great recession. The result is a heavier emphasis on security and income. This will require a different approach to what it means to take care of employees. Above all, it will require greater flexibility on the part of leaders to spend time in the organization becoming familiar with, and meeting, individual needs.

Having said this, employees of all ages seem to share one thing in common. They want to work with other good people. A reputation for excellent talent development can attract just such people.

EMPLOY TECHNOLOGY TO ENNOBLE COMPLEX JOBS AND ELIMINATE BORING JOBS

Technology can make heroes out of employees, particularly those employed in jobs in direct contact with customers, jobs that require judgment and extensive knowledge and information. Increased employee engagement follows.

Conversely, there is little point in delaying the replacement of people by technology in jobs that are boring and dispiriting. Why, for example, do we still encounter toll-takers on highways? Jobs such as these with little opportunity for advancement in skills, knowledge, or position increasingly will be eliminated, and with good riddance.

Many organizations have jobs of both types. Those employing technology selectively are at the forefront of an effort to reduce cost, improve quality, and foster the engagement of employees whose jobs not only have been preserved but improved.

GIVE EMPLOYEES LATITUDE (WITHIN LIMITS AND WITH ACCOUNTABILITY) TO DELIVER RESULTS

Delegation of authority to get work done coupled with accountability has been an important principle of leadership going back to the nineteenth century. Today it can be interpreted in terms of latitude (within limits) to deliver results delegated to employees at all levels of an organization. At Southwest Airlines, for example, the policy is "do whatever you feel comfortable doing for a Customer."[14] If you feel uncomfortable, check with a manager. Otherwise, just do it, whether you tell anyone about it or not. This has produced some extraordinary stories about service as well as devoted customers. Note, however, the word *comfortable* in the policy. It provides the limit, an element of accountability, within which latitude is granted.

This policy is at the cornerstone of the strategy employed by Châteauform', a Paris-based operator of more than thirty executive development training facilities in historic refurbished chateaus in several European countries.[15] Each venue is operated by a carefully selected couple, with latitude to maintain the chateau as they would their home and operate it to provide an outstanding experience for clients who bring groups of executives to the chateau for education in its classrooms. Visiting executives are in turn invited to feel at home in the relaxed atmosphere of the chateau. The fees are all-inclusive. In addition to studying in well-outfitted classrooms, guests engage in athletic activities or just walk the usually impressive grounds. There is a well-stocked bar but no bartender and no tab—help yourself. Food is served buffet style and left out in the kitchen for late-night snacking. The chateau dog is ready to be walked by guests.

This is do-it-yourself executive development in a special setting. Of course, it's also a relatively low-cost operating model that generates ample profit. The host couple is judged and compensated on the operating profit it delivers as well as the guest reviews and the repeat business they generate.

Care in executing this principle is required. Delegation and the provision of latitude to deliver results to others is an attractive concept. How many times have we heard that even housekeepers at a Ritz-Carlton hotel can commit the organization to a $2,000 "quick fix" of a problem for a guest? Too often, however, managers hearing this regard it as a stand-alone prescription for success. Wrong.

At a Ritz-Carlton hotel, for example, the process begins with very careful selection and hiring of new employees. A premium is placed on those with a positive attitude toward other people and a certain empathy for associates and guests. This is followed by both formal training and less formal daily training on the job, which begins on each shift with a short meeting to go over the guest list, the nature of groups staying at the hotel, and any celebrities or special events that associates should be aware of. Problems or questions are raised and addressed.

So far, so good. But Ritz-Carlton associates would not attain reputations for great service without outstanding support systems, including the guest history that tracks guests and their preferences from one Ritz-Carlton property to another. Only then— after being hired for attitude, trained for skills, and backed up with great support systems—are they entrusted with the organization's funds to correct problems that might arise among guests.

In these examples, actions are left to the employee, communicating the organization's confidence in the employee's judgment. Where the policy is successful, however, the delegation of authority is never practiced in a vacuum. Think of it as part of a recipe, not random food choices in a cafeteria. It first requires (1) hiring for attitude, (2) training for skills, and (3) providing outstanding support systems. Then and only then does latitude to deliver results work best. So remember. It's 1, 2, 3, 4—not some other sequence.

RECOGNIZE EFFORT, BUT ESPECIALLY RESULTS

It's no secret that employees like to be recognized for their effort and achievements. Styles of recognition have changed over time. For example, at one time employee-of-the-month programs were popular. They produced mixed reactions from employees, depending on the norms of the organization. Employees like to have their good work and achievements recognized, but employee-of-the-month programs don't fit well with efforts to encourage teamwork, for example. Worse yet, in organizations with ineffective cultures, winners may be regarded as "rate busters," adding to their embarrassment rather than their positive feelings about the workplace. Such programs may work better for teams than individuals.

What we are seeing instead is a steady effort to transform recognition into a more frequent act carried out quietly on the job and in the moment of achievement. It becomes part of the ongoing individual coaching process.

STAFF SPARINGLY, PAY REASONABLY

I haven't mentioned the relationship between compensation and engagement. While it's not zero, it doesn't seem to be very important, certainly not as important as what is described above. While this is true of the absolute level of compensation, periodic increases, regardless of size, do appear to provide useful support for other efforts to engage employees.

Employees will cut an organization some slack on pay if they are experiencing a great place to work. But there is no evidence that a pay advantage exists for such organizations. Instead, it is more likely that great places to work win all ties when it comes to hiring among those competing for the good talent.

Some of the most highly rated places to work, such as the regional grocery chain Publix, provide employee ownership.

This both attracts talent and fosters retention. Costco is managed with the philosophy set forth some years ago by the late David Glass, then CEO of Walmart: "Fewer, better, higher-paid employees will win every time." (Only recently has his former organization appeared to begin to adopt this philosophy.) Organizations adopting this philosophy are, by definition, demanding places to work. They may also be great places to work.

TRAIN FOR ENGAGEMENT

Employee engagement is the product of many activities—hiring, coaching, rewarding—as well as decisions and behaviors associated with the way changes of all kinds—from job assignments to promotions—are carried out by managers. It depends in large part on the trust among employees that a manager engenders in carrying out those actions. Based on what we know from those who have studied the phenomenon, we're speaking here of one's immediate boss, not necessarily the top management of an organization, which almost always scores lower than one's immediate boss on these measures.[16]

One recent study documents the impact of immediate leadership, not some abstract CEO, on the employee experience. It found, among other things, that "managers account for an astounding 70 percent of the variance in their team's engagement," and "fifty-two percent of exiting employees say that their manager could have done something to prevent them from leaving their job." Perhaps the most sobering finding of this same study was that "only 2 in 10 employees strongly agree that their performance is managed in a way that motivates them to do outstanding work."[17]

We know how to create a great place to work and how to engage employees. But we do a poor job of communicating that to managers whose most important responsibilities may be just that. Few managers I've encountered are aware of the results of studies identifying determinants of engagement. Few have experienced any formal instruction in how to do what has been described earlier in this chapter. And if they are not measured on and rewarded for engagement levels, why should they be interested in training to improve them?

One problem may be that responsibility for employee engagement is too often diffused among several functions and levels in the organization. Some assume that it's the job of the human resource department. But the HR department is often too buried in operating detail and the nuts and bolts of recruiting and training to be concerned with engagement.

Rather, this is the job of managers at all levels of the organization but especially on the front line, who researchers tell us have the greatest impact on employee engagement. The problem is that managers at this level receive little systematic training in the task. Their performance is rarely measured on yardsticks such as employee loyalty (intent to remain on the job), productivity, and ownership behaviors such as employee referrals, suggestions for better ways of doing things, or achievements requiring collaboration. Further, they are rarely judged or rewarded on the engagement levels of their charges.

Intense training time to foster engagement need not be lengthy; the lessons are not complex. Many consist only of following simple daily reminders of what employees expect of their leader. Small investments can yield significant results. Short personal interactions based on mutual trust can have a big influence on an employee's engagement and decision to remain in the organization. Social scientists can tell us a lot about how to do it.[18]

For example, one study describes an experiment involving just a two-hour orientation for new employees at WIPRO, the Indian-based call-center service support organization that was at the time experiencing a high rate of turnover. Several hundred newly hired employees received the same orientation during the first hour. During the second hour, one group received additional training focused on the company and what to expect. At the end of the hour, they received a sweatshirt with the company's logo printed on it. The second hour for the other group was focused on the new hires and how they saw themselves fitting into their jobs. At the end, each of these employees also received a personalized sweatshirt *with their name printed alongside the company's name on it*. In a surprise to the researchers, the retention rate seven months later for new hires from the second group was 2.5 times that of the retention rate for those from the first group. All it took was a one-hour orientation centered around them rather than the company, one that was memorialized by a personalized sweatshirt.[19]

The process of on-the-job practice, observation, and feedback never ends. It involves observation and real-time coaching, something that is rarely available to practicing managers. Too few leaders spend enough time on the front lines to do it.

It's one reason why middle-level managers at Walmart spend at least four days a week in the field working with store managers and becoming acquainted and interacting with employees at all levels in their respective regions.

Leading organizations stress the importance of efforts to recognize and reward employee engagement and those individuals who are good at training managers to achieve it. Their leaders recognize this as an attractive means of differentiating their organizations from their competitors—one more way of competing through culture.

DON'T ELIMINATE PRESSURE

Before we turn to other matters, let me pause to deal with a misconception that there is less pressure to perform at great places to work.

Organizations with effective cultures can be pressure cookers. *The thing that distinguishes them is that most of the pressure is created by those experiencing it.* Goals, whether explicit or implicit, are rigorous. Frontline employees are given the latitude to deliver results to customers; they'll often go out of their way to do it. Employees typically are paid well and recognized for their abilities to manage by shared values, coached when experiencing difficulties, and fired when necessary to preserve the quality of the workplace (as opposed to just "making the numbers"). Managers are cheerleaders, coaches, advocates, and coordinators. Most of the fun is work-centered and results-oriented.

It becomes visible in the form of satisfaction in winning, most often as a team.

Finally, an unusually high proportion of hires are self-selected, people who've concluded that, despite the pressure, the culture appeals to them. These are features of what Jeffrey Pfeffer terms a "sustainable" organization, one that engages its people for the long term—one that results in lower destructive stress, better family relationships, less economic inequality, better health, and even lower morbidity for employees than they might experience in an organization with an ineffective culture.[20]

GUARD AGAINST BURNOUT

The dark side of engagement, of course, is burnout. Extremes of the behaviors discussed here leading to the kinds of passion and drive that characterize engaged employees just can't be maintained. The short-term antidotes are such things as office settings that encourage break-taking, guided meditation, assistance with gym memberships, social events, and community activities outside the office. Longer-term sabbaticals may be appropriate for some, but they tend to take the individual away from the organization for too long. This can be disruptive in a rapidly growing and changing organization.

Among the best antidotes to burnout are leaders who, unlike some, recognize the problem. They exhibit the kinds of behaviors they expect in others. They set an example by visibly, and without guilt, guarding time for family and other outside activities while encouraging others to do so as well. This helps explain why—despite the unusually high demands placed on employees to produce in a great place to work—some high-performing organizations experience relatively low levels of tension, stress, and fatigue.[21]

As we will see later, an organization with an effective culture is not for everyone. In fact, for the wrong people, it can be a miserable place to work. But for the right people, it can represent the opportunity of a lifetime.

EXECUTE THE EXIT WELL

Each year, over 40 percent of workers in the United States change jobs.[22] Of these, six in ten are "quits," or voluntary departures. Employee exits are not that common in organizations with high levels of employee engagement. But well-executed exits are. The best involve exit interviews intended to identify things that might need fixing, solicitation of advice from departing employees about what could have been done better, and what the exiting employee would say to a friend or relative about what to expect on the job. Those departing involuntarily are offered assistance as part of outplacement. There is an ulterior motive for investing in this part of the relationship. For years, it has been typical in companies whose employees leave to work for customers, as in firms offering professional services. Today it has more to do with building the company brand as an employer in an age of more widely available information about various organizations as places to work. Call it the Glassdoor effect.

Founded in 2008, Glassdoor is the most frequently used of several websites to which talent can go to find information about prospective employers. (You may recall that I referenced data from Glassdoor in chapter 3.) At Glassdoor, the information is provided, among other ways, through individual reviews by current and former employees, whose ratings (on a five-point scale) of their employers are averaged into one score. One 2018 estimate was that the "site now has thirty-three million reviews of more than seven hundred thousand companies in almost two hundred countries."[23] According to one account, "Glassdoor upended workplace power dynamics" by the disclosure of information not formally available to potential employees.[24]

CEOs also are rated on Glassdoor by the percentage of employees that endorse them. More than a few CEOs with whom I'm acquainted regularly check their Glassdoor rating and compare it with others.

Such websites are criticized for their natural bias toward negative reviews, the potential for gaming through planted reviews, and influence from external effects such as layoffs and facility closings. But when thought of like a meat cleaver versus a scalpel, they can help identify organizations with functional or dysfunctional cultures, as potentially good or bad places to work. Invariably, they have given potential job applicants information on which they can base more informed questions in job interviews. And they have sensitized employers to the importance of effective workplace culture.

EXECUTE FOR THE LONG TERM

Some organizations surface as great places to work only to lose their competitive advantage in markets for talent. A change in leadership often is the reason. It remains to be seen, for example, whether the recently attained sky-high engagement levels at T-Mobile can be sustained. To be sure, competitive success awaited T-Mobile in the form of employee and customer engagement. Why? Because it led to greater concern for employees and customers (important elements of the company's strategy), higher productivity, more innovation, greater customer satisfaction and loyalty, and more financial growth and profit. Along the way, management engineered a merger with Sprint that produced a viable third competitor to Verizon and AT&T. The result has become a company whose growth and financial performance, despite clear strategic disadvantages and limited resources, is beginning to reflect what is going on with employees and customers.

After having led this successful eight-year effort, John Legere retired, going out on a high note in 2020. Now the fun from a research standpoint begins. Will T-Mobile be able to maintain its momentum?

A small number of organizations embed policies and practices whose life is longer than that of any given leader. Effective cultures and high engagement levels in organizations such as the U.S. Marines, the Mayo Clinic, Harvard Business School, and the Vanguard Group have outlasted the tenure of their respective founders and will outlast the tenure of their current leaders. Why is this assured? We get to it next.

IF YOU REMEMBER NOTHING ELSE . . .

Workplaces where employees are highly engaged are characterized by:

- Employee identification with an exciting mission, fulfilling culture, and promising business strategy.
- A policy of hiring for attitude, training for skills, providing outstanding support systems, *then* expanding employee latitude (within limits and with accountability) to deliver results—a 1, 2, 3, 4-step recipe.
- Workplace development that reflects what employees tell us:
  - Foster trust through no-surprises leadership.
  - Ensure psychological safety.
  - Hire and develop people that attract other good people.
  - Employ technology to ennoble complex jobs and eliminate boring jobs.
  - Give employees latitude (within limits and with accountability) to deliver results.
  - Recognize effort, but especially results.
  - Staff sparely and pay reasonably.
  - Train for engagement; it's generally so inadequate in most organizations that it represents an opportunity for competitive advantage.
  - Maintain good kinds of pressure, those that are created by employees themselves.
  - Provide safeguards against burnout.
  - Execute employee exits well.

Chapter Five

HOW EFFECTIVE CULTURES ARE SUSTAINED

YOU'VE PROBABLY heard the definition of arrogance: that's the U.S. Marine from Texas who graduated from Harvard Business School. However you feel about that depends on your background. But it is hard to overlook the fact that all three of these institutions, and others like the Mayo Clinic and the Vanguard Group, have succeeded because of the cultures they have sustained, at times despite criticism by others in their respective industries. There may be sharp contrasts in what these institutions do, but there are remarkable similarities in the ways they have sustained their cultures over long periods.

Some of the similarities come through in the stories that are told inside and outside these organizations. Stories of demanding training exercises or heroic deeds are told and retold wherever current or former members of the United States Marine Corps gather. They often involve unit-level actions taken in battle. They are passed from career marines to recruits. And they ensure that the traditions of the corps don't die. The Marines have persisted in the context of stories told outside the corps by members of other branches of the military (including mine), most of which make some reference to the fact that one has to be "gung ho" to be one of "those."

The values shared by citizens of Texas stand out in stories told about their independence ("Don't mess with Texas."), their resilience, the good-humored way they face the vicissitudes of life, and their live-and-let-live attitude.

Many stories at Harvard Business School concern teaching and learning by faculty and students alike. They reflect, for example, the long-held custom of meeting class under all but the most extreme circumstances. Some are about faculty driving all night to get back to Boston when flights are canceled. They involve faculty members teaching, if necessary, on crutches or medical scooters. Many involve case method classroom exchanges involving students who carefully calculate the cost of an hour of class and periodically assess the return on their investment. They may concern MBA class members who've stepped forward voluntarily at the last minute to lead a class in the absence of an ill, injured, or stranded faculty member. They help explain why HBS has retained a high global reputation over more than 110 years despite periodic shifts in the popularity of various approaches to teaching and research for management.

At the Mayo Clinic, the stories involve the efforts of a medical team to come up with a complex diagnosis and timely treatment of a difficult ailment, one that couldn't be identified at another hospital. They illustrate the emphasis on teams vs.

medical stars as well as the tradition of focusing on patient-centered (as opposed to the more common physician-centered) medicine. This is a formula that has delivered priceless medicine for more than 150 years in a fashion that may be of limited interest to doctors who prefer higher individual recognition and income regardless of their enthusiasm for the patient-centered medicine (test-diagnose-prescribe-retest, etc., in a matter of hours, not weeks) that's practiced at Mayo.

Vanguard Group stories are more likely to feature someone or a group that came up with a cost-cutting idea or a low-cost investment offering. This is a reflection of the founder, the late John Bogle, who is credited with popularizing the notion of so-called index funds requiring no conventional investment management and therefore much lower management fees than were being charged in the industry at the time of their introduction. Over time, low fees and diversification of risk (over large numbers of securities) have been shown to contribute to performance superior to most managed funds. Rewards for ideas or performance typically involve a recognition ceremony that reflects a tendency at Vanguard to avoid fanfare. The award? A five-dollar certificate for lunch in the group's galley (cafeteria). It's a repeated, symbolic reminder (in an organization with more than $7 trillion—*illion* with a *tr*—in investments on its accounts) of the importance of frugality and cost-cutting. "Crew members" don't make fun of it.[1]

These are stories meant to be handed down, part of a process of sustaining an effective culture. Invariably, they illustrate ways that individuals put their organizations ahead of their own needs. These stories can be regarded as important elements of introductory training sessions. Salesforce, for example, includes a "culture storyteller" to help new hires adapt to its culture. This is just one of the ways that, having achieved reputations for excellence in what they do and as great places to work, organizations sustain their effective cultures. There are others, starting with self-selection.

ENCOURAGE SELF-SELECTION

These organizations have strong and adaptive cultures based on a set of values and practices that support learning and change. *They are great places to work, but only for some. For certain otherwise qualified candidates, they can be a living hell.* As a result, the traditional selection system has to be turned upside down to allow qualified individuals well-informed by the recruiting process to select themselves into the organization.

In the U.S. Marines, this means attracting "The Few. The Proud" who are willing to devote years to defending their country and leading others with a common purpose. These are individuals who could, after their training, lead commercial organizations for much more income.

At HBS, it means finding those academics and highly experienced business practitioners who are comfortable putting teaching on a level with research. They do so at the risk of losing professional mobility among a group of business schools that often value research over teaching. They have to enjoy leading a discussion of business cases among up to a hundred demanding students rather than imparting wisdom and knowledge by more traditional lecturing. The school is not for everyone. Prospective faculty members need to find that out before they join the organization.

The Mayo Clinic, at least before developing campuses in other cities, relied on attracting outstanding medical practitioners—in a sense specialists/generalists—willing to move to Rochester, a pleasant but somewhat isolated town in South Central Minnesota. They work not like the stars they could be in other hospitals but rather as members of patient-centered teams, whose work is, as noted earlier, organized around the needs of the patient, not the doctor.

Those self-selecting into the Vanguard Group have to value lifestyle, in a leafy suburb of Philadelphia, over industry stardom and great wealth. They are managing investments for long-term performance, not short-term big wins. As the head of the fixed-income investments at Vanguard several years ago put it, "Our people are smart, hardworking, and ethical. . . . We don't hire people who think they are masters of the universe. Maybe we don't pay enough to encourage them!"[2]

INCENTIVES TO SELF-SELECT

Some potential employees self-select based on organizational mission and shared values. Others may need more information about how things are done. At Zappos.com, the online shoe retailer, the information is provided in a four-week training program designed to expose job candidates to the highs and lows of working at Zappos. An important vehicle for doing that is the Zappos Culture Book, comprising unedited employee statements of what Zappos' culture means to each of them. But the organization doesn't stop there. To enable prospects to self-select and the organization to avoid hiring mistakes, at the end of the first week of the training program (until the end of the program), any candidate in training for leadership is offered $2,000 plus compensation for the time they've worked if they choose to leave. The "escape incentive" ensures a good match between employee expectations and the culture of the organization. It has a positive effect on the quality of the workplace.[3]

A meta-analysis of forty such realistic "job preview" programs by Jean Phillips found that they significantly reduced employee turnover, thereby reducing recruiting and training costs. One reason is that they discourage potential hires from taking a job they may not like. But more significantly, Phillips concluded that the job preview is a kind of "vaccination" against later employee defections. By eliminating the surprise that disagreeable elements of the job might present, the job preview again builds trust through "no surprises management." Some proof of this is that the "vaccination effect" works even if the "preview" is held after an employee begins employment.[4]

A CAVEAT

The argument against too strong an emphasis on self-selection is that it leads to an organization comprised of people with similar thought processes and with too little useful debate and too few creative differences. It doesn't have to work this way, especially if the organization's values honor diversity and its shared behaviors reward independent thinking, creativity, and a willingness to share ideas and concerns.

ORGANIZE AROUND TEAMS VS. STARS

The team is a natural organizational device for sustaining an effective culture. The U.S. Marines are organized around teams and are trained to support and protect one another. At HBS, many faculty members are organized in teams with the joint responsibility for teaching courses with large enrollments and multiple sections. The faculty team prepares before class and often debriefs afterward. Because instruction involves the classroom discussion of problem cases in which students take major responsibility for the learning process, teamwork between faculty and students is an important element of the learning process as well. At the Mayo Clinic, medical practitioners are organized in teams whose members are inclined to learn from one another while diagnosing and treating complicated medical afflictions.

Teamwork succeeds or fails depending on the amount of authority and responsibility delegated to the team as well as the extent to which the team is held accountable. At Southwest Airlines, teams are organized around each flight. If a plane is late getting away from the gate, it's not the pilot's fault, the baggage handler's fault, or the gate agent's fault. It's a "team late," and the team is responsible for making sure that it doesn't happen very often. As a result, Southwest's on-time performance usually ranks among the highest in the airline industry. Very little time is wasted in finger-pointing among team members.

Strong advocates of teams emphasize the importance of keeping the team small. Small teams often get more work done because they spend less time arguing about who takes responsibility or gets credit for what. At Amazon, founder Jeff Bezos is known for his "two-pizza team" rule, which holds that teams should be small enough to be fed by two pizzas.[5]

Teams are good at selecting, training, and shaping the behaviors of new members, with much of it happening in off-hours. They are effective means of allocating work, controlling the quality of output, and ending relationships with nonperformers. Peer group pressure is an effective means of achieving much of this.

Most important for us here, teams help maintain cultures. Members remind newcomers of what got the organization to its current state of high performance through both their words and actions. When accompanied by occasional reminders of shared values and behaviors reinforced by measures and actions, a team-based organization is an important device for maintaining an organization's culture.

Organizations built around so-called stars, on the other hand, may experience difficulty in transmitting and reinforcing values and accepted behaviors.[6] For one thing, stars are too often excused from conforming to the values and behaviors shared by others. They can produce perceived inequities in everything from recognition to compensation. For another, stars tend to migrate from one organization to another and are not around long enough to help reinforce the culture even if they are aware of it or believe in it. Organizations built around stars have other strengths, but ease in sustaining culture is not one of them.

Don't get me wrong. Organizations with strong and effective cultures do produce stars. But they don't celebrate them and reward them as such. (Remember the Vanguard Group's $5 meal coupon.) As a result, the stars may be likely to leave in search of greater opportunity and renown.

STAFF FOR DIVERSITY, LEAD FOR INCLUSION

Diversity and inclusion are not just catchwords on everyone's lips. On the one hand, there is a moral imperative behind them. On the other hand, they are values encouraging practices that can provide a significant competitive advantage. One mega-study of 108 studies of the effects of cultural diversity on work in teams concluded that the teams did suffer "process" losses from conflict caused in part by diversity of backgrounds, but they were also more creative and realized greater personal satisfaction.[7] Another study of diversity policy, patent citation, and product announcement data from the three thousand largest publicly traded companies in the United States concluded that "companies with policies that encourage the retention and promotion of workers across the race, sexual orientation, and gender spectrum were more innovative and released more products."[8] An Australian study of fifty global organizations concluded that diversity enhances innovation by about 20 percent.[9]

A recent McKinsey study of top executive teams in more than a thousand organizations in fifteen countries concluded that the most diverse organizations are "more innovative—stronger at anticipating shifts in consumer needs and consumption patterns that make new products and services possible, potentially generating a competitive edge." Of equal significance is the finding that the top third of the organizations in the study are pulling away from the other two-thirds in diversity and inclusion, registering higher probabilities of being the most profitable. They are exhibiting progress in achieving greater "gender and ethnic" diversity, with both, in the opinion of the researchers, having an increasingly positive impact on bottom-line performance.[10]

Despite this evidence, too many organizations are using a leaky bucket in their approach to diversity. They lose talent with diverse backgrounds as fast as they recruit it. This results in repeated announcements of efforts to improve diversity with little progress in the proportion of those with diverse backgrounds in the organization.[11]

Staffing for diversity doesn't guarantee full benefits unless leadership is geared to provide a voice to everyone on the team, encouraging everyone to participate in the creative activities of the group. It's the team leader's responsibility to see that this happens by seeking input from everyone, watching for signs that reluctant participants are ready to contribute, discouraging the interruption of a train of thought, and recognizing everyone for their contributions. It's a skill that can be and is taught on the job but often too infrequently.

For example, instructors at the Harvard Business School utilize the case method of instruction where up to a hundred students with highly diverse backgrounds regularly discuss cases in open discussion. A substantial portion (up to half) of students' evaluations depend on their contributions to the discussions. Managing inclusion in this setting is a daunting task. Not everyone can be included in every discussion. But over time, an instructor has to assess the involvement of every student, if necessary directing questions to reluctant participants in the heat of a discussion. This is not as easy as it sounds. It requires a lot of peer-to-peer coaching among faculty members, something not often found on the typical university campus. It builds a skill many leaders could do well to emulate.

Regardless of motive, directors of major corporations are taking note of the importance of diversity and inclusion. While still an uncommon practice, CEOs of companies such as Microsoft, Uber, and FirstEnergy (an Ohio utility) now find that significant portions of their incentive compensation are based on diversity and inclusion, as measured by such things as headcount and employee evaluations.[12]

ENCOURAGE LEARNING AND INNOVATION

Engaging employees is not a simple task. Doing it in a way that encourages learning, adaptation, and innovation is especially challenging. It starts with shared values.

GET THE VALUES RIGHT

A learning organization that lives adaptation and innovation is associated with several characteristics, according to recent research. These include an emphasis on values that support diversity, transparency, and a long-term orientation; the hiring of collaborators; the provision of time for personal development and learning; and the sharing of ideas among employees and customers.[13] To these, Gary Pisano, who has studied the phenomena, would add two more: transparency and frankness. As he has put it, "When it comes to innovation, the candid organization will outperform the nice one every time. The latter confuses politeness and niceness with respect. There is nothing inconsistent about being frank and respectful."[14] These are values and behaviors that are associated with a learning organization—one that supports innovation and is capable of providing the speed and agility needed in a world of constantly changing strategies.

PROMOTE EXPERIMENTATION

"Test, then invest" is a common saying among entrepreneurs and those who finance their startups. The notion is that simple, fast, inexpensive tests in the marketplace can often increase the probability of success for ideas central to a strategy. It has always been especially relevant for retailers, whose merchandise displays offer endless opportunities for testing product placement ideas in their stores.

Learning organizations try a lot of things and keep what works. This requires a lot of testing of ideas as well as a reliance on the data that such tests produce rather than the untested opinions (too often of leaders) that often dominate decision making. In these organizations, data trumps opinion.

Firms competing on today's internet find it even more feasible to test such things as offerings, page design, and service.

For example, Booking.com, a travel website, has developed what Stefan Thomke calls an "experimentation organization" in which experimentation is an integral part of everyday life where anyone can conduct or commission a test without approval from above.[15] This requires that employees receive training in how to design and carry out experiments. The Dutch-based company conducts thousands of tests every month. Evidence from a test always outweighs executive opinion. Even the failures that tests often produce are regarded as opportunities for learning, not as costly mistakes. The only failure is a poorly-designed test—one with weak hypotheses, poor data, the lack of a control group (a baseline from which change can be measured), and careless analysis of the results. Experimentation on a large scale has worked for Booking.com. The company has employed this strategy to gain the largest share of the traffic in its industry.[16]

FOSTER INTERNAL SHARING OF BEST PRACTICES

Employees also engage in best practice exchanges in which the poorer performers learn from the best. Handelsbanken, the highly successful Swedish bank, owes a great deal of its success to an organization built on the principles of delegation, accountability, and the sharing of ideas among branches. Each month the performance of each branch on basic operating measures is shared among all branches. Everyone knows who is performing at or near the top or bottom of the pack. Top management knows that it doesn't have to remind poor performers of the need to improve. Local managers of lagging branches know that they will have to consult with their top-perform-ing colleagues to find out just what they are doing to succeed (or explain to top management why they haven't done so). And why are managers of leading branches quite willing to help? As erstwhile CEO Anders Bouven said, "Why would a top-performing branch manager help his peer—especially when their performance is openly contrasted in the league tables? Our culture—there is a sense of ownership of the entire bank, as well as the branch. There is a family feeling here despite our size . . . enough of our employees are 'refugees' from other banks—they are strong and avid gatekeepers of our culture because they've seen what it's like elsewhere."[17]

Best practice exchanges are a common occurrence at the Mayo Clinic. Compensation and other policies are carefully structured to make sure that the best performers are recognized and rewarded, not penalized, for helping their peers. In many universities, faculty members are discouraged from visiting col-leagues' classrooms. At Harvard Business School it's standard practice, with visits followed by feedback and on-the-spot fac-ulty development. It's expected by junior faculty members. One faculty member's success does not occur at another's expense.

SHARE IDEAS OUTSIDE THE ORGANIZATION

Cultures that have crossed the line from proud to arrogant often have a not-invented-here mentality. One of the remark-able constants in efforts to reshape the cultures of organizations that have reached this point is an effort by a leader to encour-age benchmarking outside the organization, even if it requires sharing good ideas with outsiders in the process. This is one way that organizations with effective cultures engage in continuous learning that supports innovation and helps sustain the culture. As we will see in chapter 7, it's one of the initiatives that Pete Coors employed to get Coors Brewing back on track.

PROVIDE TIME FOR LEARNING

If learning and teaching are activities to be encouraged, this requires that time be made available for such things. Almost since its founding, Google has freed up as much as 20 percent of its employees' time for the exploration of new ideas of possible importance to the business. At USAA, a leading purveyor of financial services, most associates are organized to work on a four-day week. This provides time on the long weekends to think and study. It enables associates at all levels to take advantage of the company's extensive educational offerings—hundreds of courses, whether related to work or simply personal development and enlightenment.

ALIGN POLICIES AND PRACTICES WITH VALUES AND BEHAVIORS

Policies and practices that aren't synchronized with values and desired behaviors can wreak real havoc in an organization. Consider what happened at Wells Fargo, a company with a rich history dating back to the stagecoach and (briefly) the Pony Express and a culture that used to be held up as an example in the banking industry. As its reputation as a high-performing bank grew, the pressures for it to continue to perform, even if it meant violating shared values, also grew. Policies and practices fell out of alignment with values and behaviors, as described in box 5.1.

BOX 5.1: Cultural misalignment at Wells Fargo

For years, Wells Fargo prided itself on putting "culture first, size second." Its culture was built around the idea of One Wells Fargo, "imagining ourselves as the customer." Its vision included the mission of helping its customers succeed financially. This vision was supported by values such as "people as a competitive advantage, ethics, and what's right for customers." The organization even had gone so far as to define its culture as "understanding our vision and values so well that you instinctively know what you need to do when you come to work each day."* That's all pretty impressive. And it contributed to an industry-leading reputation for the banking giant.

Given this context, it makes sense that incentives were put in place several years ago to encourage frontline employees to develop deeper relationships—defined by the number of the bank's services utilized—with existing customers. However, the goals on which the incentives were based were somewhat daunting—so daunting that customer relationship managers began feeling pressure from above to meet what appeared to be impossible goals. Their choices? Report numbers that fell short of goals, try to have the goals reduced, or find a way—any way—to meet the numbers. Perhaps because the tradition of industry-leading performance at the bank was so deeply embedded in the culture or because lucrative incentive bonuses hung in the balance, they succumbed to the temptation to cheat. They condoned the practices of establishing fake new

---

accounts and even transferring token amounts of funds between these accounts without customers' knowledge. When the practice became so prevalent that it began to generate numerous customer complaints, it was disclosed in September 2016 that some 5,300 employees had been fired. The action was taken by leaders at the top of the organization, claiming they were unaware of the practice—leaders who themselves eventually lost their jobs, too. The monetary cost to Wells Fargo in penalties and fines has been substantial. Replacing 5,300 employees proved to be expensive in terms of hiring, training, and productivity losses. (In fact, some were hired back later.) Repairing customer relationships and replacing lost business will take time and money. And costs measured in terms of damage to the organization's reputation and culture will be substantial. Restoring trust within the organization, let alone with customers, will take some time and effort.

Much of this happened because the alignment between Wells Fargo's culture and its policies and processes was broken. The signals sent by Wells Fargo's rigorous retail banking goals and the incentive programs and disciplinary actions that accompanied them were out of step with the bank's mission and values. They must have represented unwelcome surprises to thousands of the bank's employees.

wellsfargo.com, accessed November 1, 2016. Facts in this description of what happened at Wells Fargo are presented in many publications. One of the best accounts is by Justin Peters, "How Wells Fargo Became Synonymous With Scandal," *Slate*, November 28, 2020, slate.com

Lou Gerstner, IBM's former CEO, observed in connection with the Wells Fargo problems that "Culture . . . forms as a result of signals employees get from the corporate processes that structure their priorities."[18] At Wells Fargo, the signals allegedly led to cheating and even fraud. Whether culture influences or responds to management processes—compensation practices, the short- or long-term focus of financial reporting, human resource management policies, and resource allocation—will continue to be debated. However, Gerstner's comments underline the importance of aligning an organization's culture with its policies and processes. Once that is done, the likelihood of a culture's effectiveness in supporting a strategy increases.

TAMP DOWN ENDEMIC ORGANIZATIONAL CONFLICT

Recently, a whistleblower complaint blamed the failure of the control system leading to two fatal crashes of the Boeing 737 Max jet plane on a refusal by management to honor an engineering request for a safety device. The complaint raised a concern about a corporate culture that had begun to place a priority on profit over safety. It described an organizational climate in which a "fear of retaliation" existed among those calling the matter's attention to management.[19] These are some of the worst things anyone could say about a proud producer of some of the safest products in the world.

Somewhat similar charges were lodged in the case of cheating on vehicle emissions technology at Volkswagen described earlier. And going back years before that, we experienced the failure of the O-ring on the Challenger rocket, a variation on the same theme. The human and economic costs of these failures have been astronomical. They have eerie similarities. First, they were all characterized in the press as failures of organizational culture. Second, they involved failure (and even fear) by engineers to communicate with general managers—a lack of voice that we discussed in chapter 4. But most importantly, they were manifestations of inherent differences of background, training, and interests between managers and engineers who harbored a lack of understanding and even respect for one another. Each of these failures is important on its own. When combined, they can produce ugly, even lethal, outcomes.

Inherent organizational conflict takes many forms—for example, between home office staff people ("who don't understand how the business really works," according to those in the field) and those in operating jobs ("who don't understand the big picture," according to those at headquarters), between officers and enlisted personnel in the military, between doctors and hospital administrators, and between faculty and school administrators.

This is an oversimplification of a complex phenomenon, with nuances in every organization. Such conflict is inevitable. But it is minimized in great places to work in a variety of ways. For example, at Harvard Business School, many faculty members not only serve in the classroom but also hold administrative jobs. It's easier to span organizational boundaries and minimize friction and wasted time when you've served "in the other person's shoes." At Cemex, the global building materials company, the company expends an unusually large amount of money for travel to bring far-flung managers and engineers together for both decision-making and educational activities. In other organizations where teams are important, such as at Mayo Clinic or T-Mobile, a lot of thought is given to putting teams together in ways that bring people with varying jobs and backgrounds into close contact.

FOSTER BOUNDARY-SPANNING BEHAVIORS

Leaders have a natural tendency to want to retain their best performers. This is especially true if the group they are leading is competing for performance against other groups in the organization. The challenge is to create incentives for them to share their best talent and ideas with others outside their teams. Thus, at General Electric in the 1990s under Jack Welch, leaders were judged in part on the degree to which they exhibited "boundaryless" behaviors, such as developing talent for and sharing it with other parts of the organization.

Satya Nadella eliminated a stack-ranking system of performance management at Microsoft when he assumed the leadership in 2014. Under this system, leaders were forced to rank their employees on five levels—top, good, average, below average, or poor. Ten percent of their team had to be ranked poor. This discouraged employees from sharing good ideas that others could utilize to push them down further into the stack. In other words, it discouraged boundary-spanning behaviors.

SUPPORT TEAM-BASED COMMUNITY SERVICE

Some organizations make time for executives to engage in community service. Others loan out executives for government service. Team-based community activities can provide important vehicles for getting employees together in worthwhile causes off the job. They confirm an organization's commitment to giving back, an attraction to many talented prospective employees.

They provide a rationale for organizing employees into teams that can be identified with the organization even off the job. As a result, research suggests that they contribute to an organization's economic performance and are a good investment, assuming the cause appeals to large numbers of employees and fits with the organization's values.

For example, since 1988 Rockport shoes has been a sponsor of City Year, the organization that brings together young people for at least a year at a time to work in groups on projects involving community improvement. Jeffrey Swartz, who later became president and CEO, tells the story of the badly written note that launched the project. It went, in part, "We can save the world. All we lack is 50 pairs of boots. You have lots of boots, we don't have any, please send some."[20] The fact that Rockport began putting boots on the feet of City Year teams was a source of satisfaction to company employees. But the real benefit to the organization was employee involvement working with City Year teams.

This helps explain why Google sponsors Google Week, during which thousands of its employees carry out community improvement projects organized and supervised by HandsOn Bay Area, a volunteering clearinghouse that matches volunteers to projects on which it also provides leadership throughout the San Francisco Bay Area. The company regards it as an investment with a high return, measured in terms of employee commitment.

Salesforce has one of the most extensive programs to support community involvement. It has been expanded with the success of the company and will change. At the time I write this, employees are encouraged and paid to be out of the office for up to seven days each year to provide fifty-six hours of community service, in groups or individually. Sign up and receive a chit for $2,500 to be donated to the charity of your choice. Complete fifty-six hours and receive another chit for $2,500. Go above and beyond the fifty-six hours and become a candidate to receive a chit for another $10,000. It is integral to one of the company's five success hacks: "Give employees a purpose beyond profits."[21]

Rockport, Google, and Salesforce use this as a way to illustrate the importance of giving back, a value they share. These efforts are all intended to help sustain the strong and vibrant cultures that characterize the companies. They are elements of more comprehensive programs to preserve employee engagement and commitment. The evidence that they work is collected periodically in the form of what has come to be known as employee engagement surveys. But let's get back down to earth here. Based on my research, I would bet that they more than pay for themselves, benefitting shareholders handsomely.

ORGANIZE FOR CULTURE QUALITY CONTROL—THE CULTURE OMBUDSMAN

Organizations with both strong cultures and high levels of engagement can benefit from having a person or group responsible for such things as (1) maintaining the culture by filtering ideas for everything from strategy implementation to celebrations of success, (2) managing a confidential hotline designed to field complaints about employees or situations that appear to be violating organizational values and shared beliefs about acceptable behaviors, and (3) administering the organization's climate or engagement survey. The person or group may be called many things but functions much like a culture ombudsman through which ideas, complaints, and other feedback may flow to management. This notion is in its infancy, but it offers promise.

In some cases, the function may be limited to the design and sponsorship of companywide celebrations, important artifacts in an organization's culture. For example, almost since its founding, Southwest Airlines has utilized a culture committee to organize and monitor planned events such as "three signature moments . . . Valentine's Day (aligned with our Servant's Heart), Southwest Birthday (aligned with our Warrior Spirit), and Halloween (aligned with our FUN-LUVing attitude)" plus culture blitzes in fifteen Southwest stations each year to "appreciate every Employee in that city with a fun event."[22] Committee members ensure that the events are organized and carried out in a way that reflects the company's values. The committee is one of the responsibilities of a senior vice president, culture and communications, who reports directly to the CEO.

The culture ombudsman thrives on independence from the operating functions of an organization. Ideally, it involves a reporting relationship to a senior executive with general management responsibilities. A perception of independence is important, for example, in the operation of a confidential hotline and the subsequent actions it might trigger. The need for objectivity in providing reactions to proposals for events or even strategic moves that might impact the organization's culture suggests that the ombudsman be located outside the purview of, say, marketing, finance, operations, or human resources.

Too often, responsibilities carried out by a culture ombudsman are delegated to a human resource organization entrusted
with the tasks of helping build and maintain an organization's
talent base while providing personnel support services. It is an
important set of tasks. But its orientation doesn't lend itself to
playing the role of the ombudsman. As a result, the ombudsman's role may get lost in the welter of other activities, it loses its
objectivity in the eyes of employees, and it doesn't have the credibility or top management visibility required to influence action.

MEASURE AND ACT AT ALL LEVELS
OF THE ORGANIZATION

Any organization worth its salt today measures what has come
to be called employee engagement on at least an annual basis
using customized or standardized survey questions. (Remember MarketCo's employee engagement index from chapter 3.)
Organizations utilizing standard measures can compare their
results with those from other organizations in ways that suggest
how much room there is for improvement. This is where the
problems begin.

MEASURE

First and foremost, too much reliance is placed on the engagement survey as the sole tool for maintaining a culture. Too many
engagement surveys contain items that have not been proven
to have any relationship with an organization's performance.

Results are not linked to inputs in ways that would enable improvement based on focused effort. Results are obtained and discussed with managers and even employees, but little is done about problem areas. Worse yet, the engagement survey is not related to such things as a company's mission, values, hiring criteria, performance evaluation processes, recognition, or rewards.

When it comes to the health of a culture, most organizations measure the wrong things. In the research I describe in chapter 3, to put a monetary value on culture, I had to bring too many of my own estimates to the process. Critical pieces of information were not being collected.

We measure financial performance to the last penny while neglecting important measures of cultural performance. At a minimum, what should we be measuring? I've provided a list below. If tracked periodically, items on the list provide the basis for corrective action if it is needed. They become an essential element in a kind of balanced scorecard of financial and nonfinancial measures that have become popular in many organizations.[23]

IMPORTANT MEASURES OF A CULTURE'S PERFORMANCE

- Employee loyalty, measured by voluntary turnover rates
- Customer loyalty, measured by some form of repeat business or "share of pocketbook"
- Employee trust levels, measured by trust of one's immediate boss as well as top management

- Employee inclusion, measured by whether employee voice is heard
- Employee engagement, measured by satisfaction with, and intent to remain on, the job
- Employee ownership, measured by suggested hires, ideas, products
- Customer ownership, measured by new process and product suggestions as well as new business referrals

Behaviors can be observed and measured. The purpose is to determine whether a leader, regardless of whether he or she is "making their numbers" or not, can lead using the shared values of the organization. The best observer of this is the person being led. This measurement is often obtained through the vehicle of a 360-degree feedback exercise in which those being led, peers, and others assess a leader's behavior.

Too subjective you say? It is subjective, but repeated comments from several sources lend some credibility to the feedback. And who is in the best position to judge, the leader being measured or the person being led? Another criticism is that when peers and others are protected by confidentiality, they use 360-degree feedback to unfairly air prejudices or employ language that is neither respectful nor helpful. This can happen, for example, if insufficient effort is made to prepare members of the organization for such an exercise.

Too often, performance measurement systems look as if they were designed by someone in outer space. They bear little resemblance to either the values of the organization or the behaviors that everyone agrees reflect those values. Every effort must be made to purge the process of irrelevant measures that encourage feedback that is unhelpful to the recipient. Strip it down to the least number of most relevant measures possible, with at least one measure for each of the values shared by members of the organization.

ACT

Measurement without action is a great way to scuttle the success of a lot of effort that precedes it. If there is no intent or ability to act promptly on observed and measured behaviors, it is better not to measure at all. Without follow-up action, the entire effort to shape a culture can be an unproductive use of time.

What we're talking about here in many instances is the willingness to identify and take corrective action with those who, as observed by those around them, can't or won't lead in ways that reflect shared values and behaviors. Actions may include immediate dismissal but are more likely to involve some kind of grace period to allow for possible improvement.

In committing to act, one test is whether you are prepared to require counseling or retraining for someone who is meeting financial targets but not acting according to the shared values of the culture. A bigger test is whether you are willing to let them go if they are unable to change. A gutsy decision? Yes. But based on experiences I've observed time and again, expect a boost in morale and higher productivity among associates of the departing person who witnessed the acts of mismanagement. And expect more revenue and greater profit than before.

FINALLY . . .

Maintaining an effective culture requires a mix of constant leadership vigilance, careful hiring and orientation, policies that encourage shared values and behaviors, careful measurement, and a willingness to act quickly when measures raise warning signals. This sounds complex, and it is. Fortunately, cultures tend to reinforce and self-correct themselves through the efforts of a core of strong believers throughout the organization, people who act as if they have an ownership stake, whether financial or not.

Can an effective culture and the employee engagement it supports be maintained in the face of increasing numbers of people working remotely on a full-time basis? It's a question of growing importance, one we address next.

IF YOU REMEMBER NOTHING ELSE . . .

- To attract the people necessary to sustain an effective culture, make it easy for people to self-select into or out of the organization.
- Organizations sustain effective, innovative cultures through many of the following means:
  - Telling and retelling stories that reinforce the culture
  - Encouraging self-selection
  - Organizing around teams vs. stars
  - Staffing for diversity; leading for inclusion

- o Encouraging learning and innovation through shared values as well as constant experimentation to test ideas, internal sharing of best practices, benchmarking against other organizations, and setting aside time for learning and reflection
- o Aligning policies and practices with values and behaviors
- o Tamping down endemic organizational conflict
- o Fostering boundary-spanning behavior
- o Supporting team-based community service
- o Organizing for culture quality control led by a culture ombudsman
- o Measuring managerial behaviors and taking action to encourage adherence to shared values at all levels of the organization

- The message of this chapter can be summed up in one sentence. Constant, consistent, and relevant measurement and subsequent action in the context of a comprehensive set of efforts to demonstrate and communicate "how and why we do things around here" help sustain an effective culture.

Chapter Six

CULTURE, ENGAGEMENT, AND WORK FROM ANYWHERE

THE TREND toward remote work was reinforced by the COVID-19 virus pandemic, which required full-time remote work in many parts of the world and introduced many to the advantages of working at home at least part of the time.[1] Remember, we're talking about full-time remote work as opposed to part-time telecommuting that brings employees to a central office for some part of each week. After COVID-19, there is a likelihood that many employees will find remote work so feasible and attractive that they will not want to return to an office. Facebook, for example, was one of the first large organizations to confirm this notion, announcing that half of its employees could be working remotely in the next decade. As founder Mark Zuckerberg put it, "It's clear that Covid has changed a lot about our lives, and that certainly includes the way that most of us work."[2]

Several recent studies suggest that remote work isn't working for everyone and hint at what can be done about it. A 2020 survey by Finance Buzz, for example, found that 46 percent of team members working remotely felt isolated from other team members, 37 percent missed face time with managers or company leaders, and 29 percent found it challenging to collaborate with their colleagues. Nevertheless, 81 percent of those expressing concerns wanted to continue to do work remotely, primarily because of greater flexibility in working from anywhere and scheduling work as well as time saved from commuting.[3] This kind of data has led one commentator to conclude that it is necessary for "a virtual culture" to "drive a sense of purpose with over-communication."[4]

If an effective culture can enhance remote work, then remote work surely increases the value of an effective culture. But how do you sustain a culture that fosters engagement and its benefits in a world trending increasingly toward tech-supported remote work?[5] That was a challenge facing Dianne Wilkins, CEO of Critical Mass (CM), a digital experience design agency based in Calgary, Canada. Long before the outbreak of the pandemic, Wilkins's organization was in the process of creating an organized approach to expanding remote work as part of an effort to address the belief that "our greatest threat for years to come centers on talent." As a result, CM sought to expand its talent pool, eliminating the hiring issue of job location by expanding remote work.[6]

All well and good. But CM is an organization with a culture regarded as very special by its employees. As CEO Wilkins put it, "You're likely to meet your new set of best friends when you join Critical Mass." In a sense, Wilkins was confronting two questions: What's the future of remote work? How will it affect our ability to maintain an outstanding organizational culture at CM?

There was no question that some of the company's work could be performed remotely. Sara Anhorn, executive vice president of talent at CM, commented, "People want a different way of working. . . . People with the type of talent we need at Critical Mass live everywhere, not just near where we have different plans to open (an office)." New technology could make it possible for them to interact with others working remotely or not.

Wilkins was confident that her organization could deal with issues such as remote worker isolation, "second-class citizenship," and the problem of "finding" remote workers when necessary. But the most difficult issue was whether CM's special culture could be preserved. Her organization had something going for it that suggested potential success. As she put it, "It was a blinding flash of the obvious that an experience design agency should (be able to) design a holistic employee experience at its core rather than a set of related but separate processes and programs." In short, she believed that if anybody could maintain a competitive culture in the face of increasing remote work, CM would be able to do it.

Wilkins's response was to organize an effort called Liquid, a carefully designed strategy (described in box 6.1) to integrate work performed in an office and by those working full time from anywhere else. In doing so, she benefitted from the experiences of other organizations further along in converting to work performed from anywhere. Her organization learned some important lessons about the extra care needed in hiring those "buying in" to the notion, the difficulties of building a community, challenges of performing creative work in teams typically carried out around a whiteboard, efforts required to ensure that workers outside don't "get lost," and the inadequacy of most middle management training when it comes to leading those not working from the office. But I'll let her tell about it in box 6.1.

BOX 6.1: Critical mass: preserving organization culture in a remote workforce

---

Founded in 1996, Critical Mass (CM) by 2019 had grown to 950 employees organized around twelve offices in several countries. The Calgary-based company designs digital experiences for a wide range of clients. It has been faced with the challenge of competing for talent in a changing world of professional service work. As CEO Dianne Wilkins said, "Our greatest threat for the years to come centers on talent." CM's executive vice president of talent, Sara Anhorn, added, "Talent is changing. Many people can't wait to abandon traditional workplace models." Nearly 10 percent of CM's employees were working remotely on a full-time basis as Wilkins and her team began in 2018 to develop a strategy for preserving a special organization culture while accommodating increases in remote work.

The CM Culture

According to Sara Anhorn, "The connective tissue at CM is our culture . . . grounded in our six long-held values:

> Honest . . . Tell the truth & make courageous choices.
> Inspired . . . Listen & engage.
> Driven . . . Never stop trying.
> Purposeful . . . Make the world a better place.

Real . . . Never be fake.

Equal . . . Treat each other as equals—always.

We have woven them . . . purposely into everything we do."

The values are integrated into the interview scripts used to screen candidates. At work, associates are encouraged to call out colleagues whose behaviors don't reflect the values. The effort encompasses such things as coaching by career developers assigned to each associate; frequent personal feedback; and recognition awards, shout-outs, and spot bonuses for actions reflecting CM's values. It's reflected in workplace design, with posters featuring the values in all of the meeting rooms. By 2018 it was clear to management that CM's culture was an important factor in its recent rapid growth and success. Nevertheless, CM was losing associates due to an inability to meet substantial salary and remote work offers from competitors. The question was, could the culture be preserved and associate retention rates even improved with the prospect of more remote work? CM's answer was a strategy and set of initiatives called Liquid.

Liquid

Liquid is an initiative launched in the fall of 2018. Why Liquid? CM's leaders avoid the use of the word *remote* because they expect teams with some all-remote associates to be inclusive. Liquid is based on CM's experience with full-time remote work and a great deal of best practice research in other organizations. The goals set for Liquid are to expand the company's talent pool while preserving as much of the culture as possible while achieving some remote work productivity increases by eliminating commuting time and avoiding the feeling of "second-class citizenship" among "Liquids." It has involved the testing of several ideas, including the establishment of mini-hubs—clusters of remote workers without company offices— and requiring all in-office associates to work at home one day a week to sensitize them to what Liquid workers are experiencing.

Special efforts have included the creation of a portal containing a popular program called Critical Start followed by ninety-day periodic check-ins, as well as the development of a Liquid talent policy, a manual to guide remote workers and those managing them. Interview guides have been expanded to assess potential candidate self-motivation and engagement. A tool called Match has been built to fit all associates and their talent profiles with task assignments and job opportunities.

New Liquid talent is flown to designated core offices for project kick-offs. Teams are encouraged to build virtual relationships using the organization's software and apps like Slack. Individuals are paired with career developers and encouraged to meet virtually with them weekly. Everyone participates in weekly office town halls via Webex. In addition, monthly Liquid meetings are organized by office to share lessons learned. All are brought back to their core offices for an annual meeting with their career developers, other Liquids, and counterparts not working remotely. Virtual "Beer O'Clocks"—happy hours on Slack—have even been attempted on Fridays.

All of this has required added training for managers, regardless of their work location. Required training ranges from topics like how to make effective use of CM's communication and other technology to ways of ensuring that Liquid associates have a voice and are included in all company activities.

Thanks in part to Liquid, thus far Wilkins and her team appear to have met goals set for the initiative—to be able to preserve associate satisfaction and engagement levels while improving associate retention rates. Potential improvements are being tested constantly. Lessons learned thus far include:

In selecting those working remotely, don't be too impressed by effective communicators vs. those promising to be a good social fit.

Never consider anyone who hints they might detract from the culture.

Certain activities lend themselves to remote work better than others. At CM, creative work typically performed around a whiteboard has proved challenging.

The biggest challenge of remote work may be in building a sense of community.

The CM team is still trying to figure out how to make "Beer O'Clock" work without having it feel "awkward or forced."

A comprehensive remote work strategy requires extra coaching for midlevel managers in leading remote workers if an organization's culture is to be preserved.

Source: This box is based on Dan Maher and Dan O'Brien, "The Future Came Early and It's Liquid: Critical Mass (A) and (B)" Omnicom University Case Nos. OU-228A and OU228B, respectively, Omnicom Group, Inc., 2020. Its content is used with the permission of management.

HOW ALL-REMOTE ORGANIZATIONS DO IT

Organizations such as Automattic and GitLab have, among other things, dealt with the issue of second-class citizenship for remote workers by converting to an all-remote format, shutting down their executive offices. These are organizations whose businesses, software as a service, are based largely on coding work that lends itself to working remotely. They deal in technology, so they should be especially adept at using it to foster a sense of community, promote productivity, and effectively hand off work among people working on an asynchronous basis around the globe. And they have been able to grow exponentially while seeking to achieve these things.

To make all-remote strategies work, let alone preserve cultures that support employee and customer engagement, leaders of these organizations have found that it takes extra effort to communicate across their organizations, ensure that middle managers (the key to remote work success) are doing the same, gather people on a face-to-face basis from time to time, and make sure that employees working remotely don't "fall off the grid" and become difficult to engage.

For example, Automattic, "the company behind WordPress, which powers 35 percent of all websites on the Internet," had by 2020 reached $3 billion in value while operating with more than 1,200 employees working asynchronously in seventy-five countries and no office.[7] Under founder Matt Mullenweg, the company has given as much thought to operating an all-remote strategy as any. Mullenweg has set forth five levels of operating effectiveness for such strategies (see box 6.2) and judges his company as operating at level four, which he describes from the remote employee's standpoint as "I'll get to it when it suits me," a euphemism for empowering remote employees to do what they feel necessary to preserve quiet time for productive, creative work, including the management of intrusive, often unnecessary communications from colleagues. To facilitate this, the company deploys the latest in communications technology (including a WordPress plugin called P2, which acts as an internal blog and simulates water-cooler-idea exchanges) as well as such things as strict meeting discipline to foster employee productivity. Asynchronous work plus a heavy emphasis on written communication enables employees to hand off work to one another, spend extended periods in uninterrupted creative work, and take time to compose thoughtful responses to queries from colleagues.

An all-remote (or as Mullenweg prefers to call it, "distributed") work strategy requires a conscious effort to bring remote workers together. At Automattic, that means four weeks out of the year for team bonding and team building events. In

BOX 6.2 The Five Levels of Remote Work

Level One: "No deliberate action"—smartphone and email;
dial in to a few meetings

Level Two: "Re-creating the office online"—think
synchronous work, unnecessary meetings, interruptions,
and real-time communication, except it's now online

Level Three: "Adapting to the medium"—synchronous work
using shared documents and charts as well as better
meeting discipline and equipment to improve team
work

Level Four: "Asynchronous communication"—a rewarding
culture supported by state-of-the-art technology and
characterized by improved productivity, effective hand
offs, and time to focus and create

Level Five: "Nirvana"—a culture that works better than any
in-person company ever could

Source: Steve Glaveski, "The Five Levels of Remote Work: And Why You're
Probably at Level 2," Medium.com, March 29, 2020, https://medium
.com/swlh/the-five-levels-of-remote-work-and-why-youre-probably-at
-level-2-ccaf05a25b9c.

addition, it means that employees have to have the best technology in their home workspaces; for example, Automattic supplies
proper lighting and background sound muffling devices for
video communication. To ensure network security, devices such
as employee laptops and cell phones are shielded from hackers.

There is a question of whether all-remote organizations can
grow successfully beyond a certain size and preserve their cultures. Both Automattic and GitLab, for example, employ no
more than two thousand people. Sid Sijbrandij, CEO of GitLab,

takes issue with that belief. He has said, "I think all-remote scales even better than the traditional model . . . the benefits of all-remote: writing down your processes, stimulating cross-company informal communication, they get more pronounced at scale."[8]

THE IMPORTANCE OF MIDDLE MANAGEMENT IN A WORK-FROM-ANYWHERE STRATEGY

Middle managers are the water carriers of an organization's culture, regardless of whether it is pursuing a work-from-anywhere strategy or not. It is true of all the organizations featured in this chapter. It requires more than just recognition and lip service. Middle managers have to be trained to represent the organization and its culture to those working remotely, to make every effort to understand the idiosyncratic needs of each person working remotely under their supervision, to serve as effective communications conduits, to avoid unnecessarily disturbing those engaged in creative remote work, and to ensure that top management is aware of what is happening on the front lines of the organization.

According to William Horner, business culture analyst at WCM Investment Management, a firm that values corporate culture in its investment decisions, a critical feature of firms employing remote strategies successfully is "a strong backbone of mid-upper level leaders who proactively reach out to (remote) employees and stay in touch to provide some cohesiveness and prevent people from feeling out of the loop or disconnected from the 'heartbeat' of the organization."[9]

MIXING OFFICE-BASED AND REMOTE EMPLOYEES

Dianne Wilkins had no aspirations to convert Critical Mass to an all-Liquid workforce. Her goal was to preserve her organization's culture while accommodating larger numbers of remote workers. Of greater relevance for her and her colleagues at Critical Mass were the experiences of organizations with only a portion of their people working remotely. Firms such as Deloitte (management consulting), Schlumberger (petroleum exploration), and ISS (cleaning and other services) have for years performed most of their work in the field, whether in teams (where peer group pressure can help preserve a culture) or individually. An old saying about culture applies especially to Danish-based ISS's night-shift office cleaners: "Culture is what happens when no one is looking."[10] These organizations also have found that extra effort—more frequent communication, social gatherings, and opportunities for individual feedback and counseling—has to be put forth by leadership to create highly regarded places to work and retain employees. As we've noted, this is especially true for middle managers, often team leaders in those organizations.

Back at Critical Mass, the first-year results for Liquid were encouraging. Employee satisfaction and engagement figures all held steady (although sources of satisfaction for Liquid associates may have been different than for their nonremote colleagues). Productivity increased slightly. Employee retention, which had been about average for the industry, improved. New ideas for engaging remote workers were being tested. And the challenges of fostering collaborative creative work, creating less artificial social experiences remotely, and perhaps most important of all, added "coaching for people who manage Liquid employees"—were being addressed. Little did CM's leadership know that one year after the launch of Liquid a massive pandemic would sweep the world and make remote work necessary. Because of Liquid, the company was able to take the black swan event in stride. It gave them a head start on many other organizations forced to change their thinking about remote work in the future.

WHAT WE HAVE LEARNED THUS FAR

Based on the experiences of a wide variety of firms doing different kinds of work, one can only conclude that maintaining an effective culture in a world of increasingly remote work will be a real challenge, but it can be achieved.

It will be increasingly important to attain and maintain the sense of community that most remote workers seek. Can the equivalent of the water cooler be created? How about the equivalent of collaborative creative work around the whiteboard? Can communications technology improve in ways that emulate the social interaction that people craved for and missed during the COVID-19 pandemic? Regardless of whether technology can fill this gap, organizations will have to budget differently. Expect any savings in real estate costs for unneeded office space to be spent for extra leadership training, employee travel, and organized gatherings to bring remote workers together with others. Further, promotion opportunities will have to be opened up to those working remotely. "Out of sight, out of mind" can't be the modus operandi.

Based on the anecdotal evidence we have so far, the best that leaders of increasingly remote workforces can hope for may be hiring advantages and modest increases in productivity without losses in levels of employee satisfaction, engagement, and loyalty to the organization. But it will take a different allocation of leadership time and effort to ensure that extra attention is devoted to those working remotely.

IF YOU REMEMBER NOTHING ELSE . . .

- A crisis such as the COVID-19 pandemic has stimulated interest in remote work strategies and may provide extra impetus to a trend already underway.
- There are as many remote work strategies as there are competitive situations; many can put added strain on an organization's culture. They range from work performed by a minority of employees working remotely and with common (synchronous) hours to a so-called all-remote work strategy in which there is no office, no synchronous working hours, and work that is handed off from one time zone to another.
- A hybrid strategy, with a portion of a workforce working remotely, can pose a particular challenge of maintaining first-class citizenship for those working remotely.
- Remote work strategies require extra effort and ingenuity—a kind of doubling down on the efforts described earlier in this book—on the part of the organization's leadership at all levels if the culture is to be preserved.

- An important element required to maintain a culture in a remote work strategy is middle management. Extra training may be required. New roles, such as that of the career developer for each remote worker, may have to be created.
- The goal of a remote work strategy should not be cost savings. Instead, savings realized in the real estate costs to maintain office space will be spent on efforts to bring remote workers together periodically and train middle managers in how best to manage remotely.
- When assessing the impact of remote work strategies on organizational culture, a reasonable goal is the maintenance of levels of job satisfaction, engagement, and employee loyalty with modest increases in productivity and substantial advantages in attracting talent.

Chapter Seven

CHANGE THE CULTURE

PETER COORS, then the president of Coors Brewing Company, once told me a story I've never forgotten as we sat in his office in Golden, Colorado, some thirty years ago. I was there because a sample of brewing industry executives, competitors of Coors, had identified the company as having the strongest culture in the industry in a research study John Kotter and I were conducting at the time.[1] Despite this, the company's performance had lagged the industry for several years. I was there to learn how such a strong culture could be associated with such poor performance.

The story concerns a time in the early 1980s when Coors beer was distributed only in the western United States. In those days before the rise of microbreweries, its beer had an almost mythical character, reflecting the company's legendary dedication to quality. Travelers visiting from the eastern United States would take home six-packs of Coors to share with their best friends.

Somehow an explanation for Coors' regional distribution began to circulate. It went like this: because the company carefully controlled the temperature at which its beer was distributed, there was a concern that a long and complex shipment to the east posed a possible quality risk. Whether true or not, it added to the mystique surrounding the beer.

Those were rough-and-tumble days at Coors, reflecting another aspect of the company's culture that honored the values of the Old West. Disputes among executives were settled in the parking lot on a "may-the-best-man-win" basis. The practice was discontinued only when a senior executive suffered injuries that required he go to the hospital emergency room.

There were other problems as well. Ironically, several grew out of the sense of pride in producing the best beer in America— a reflection of the strongest corporate culture in the industry, according to competitors. The pride, however, had turned to arrogance. One example serves to illustrate the point.

At about this time, Coors began packaging its beer in a newly designed can. There was only one problem. Customers were reporting that they found the can difficult to open. An airline cabin attendant would attempt unsuccessfully to open the can, finally handing it to a passenger for assistance. Coors distributors were becoming upset; the product was being returned, and customers were asking for the old can. The situation became so dire that several distributors in Southern California met and decided to send one of their number, former world record holder and 1960 Olympian discus silver medal winner Richard Aldrich "Rink" Babka—today in his eighties, still a formidable six feet five and 267 pounds—to Golden to argue their case and find a solution.

According to Pete Coors, he was joined in the meeting with Babka by another senior Coors executive. After Babka had pleaded his case, the executive leaned across the table and said, "You don't understand, Rink. We make the best beer in the country; people will find a way to get to it." Whereupon Babka circled the table, grabbed the Coors executive by the lapels, and said, "What you don't understand, Tom, is that you're putting us out of business." Coors had to step in and say, "Rink, let Tom go and we'll talk about this."

The moment called for something to be done about a culture that had become dysfunctional. The signs that this was happening were the typical ones. They included (1) a tendency to assume that the practices that had produced success in the past would once again foster strong performance; (2) a strong sense of pride that had turned to arrogance toward customers, suppliers, and others; (3) the commonly held notion that there was little to learn from competitors or other firms regarded as leaders in their respective industries; (4) a lack of internal support for sharing best practices and learning in general; and (5) an inbred management that rejected new ideas and those who might bring them to the organization.

It was time for action. And what Pete Coors did is memorable. We'll return to it later.

SYMPTOMS THAT THINGS ARE GOING DOWNHILL

As Coors, Wells Fargo (See box 5.1), and other examples illustrate, effective cultures can stagnate. The symptoms that this is happening include (1) a forgotten mission, values, or behaviors among leaders of the organization; (2) increasing instances in which people fail to do what they say they will do; (3) a resulting lack of trust among members of the organization; (4) avoidance of constructive confrontation; (5) a tendency to take consensus-based decision making to an extreme; (6) an inability to make and execute decisions quickly; (7) gossip, but inaction concerning leaders failing to adhere to shared values and behaviors; (8) behaviors that many members of the organization would regard as unethical; and (9) ultimately, increasing numbers of defections at all levels of the organization.

To this list, I would add one more, thanks to Travis Kalanick, the deposed CEO of Uber who lost his job because his behavior was perceived as violating the company's values and accepted behaviors. He wrote, in an unpublished letter that surfaced later, that some of the values he had championed for the company's culture had become "weaponized." They were encouraging destructive behaviors. Frances Frei and Anne Morriss, in their insightful book, have picked up on this and defined a weaponized value as "the manipulation of an espoused value to disempower, or in extreme cases, harm someone."[2] For example, the value of meritocracy at Uber was said to be used to justify what one observer described as "a Hobbesian environment at the company in which workers are sometimes pitted against one another and where a blind eye is turned to infractions from top performers."[3] It's another reminder to keep our eyes on the behaviors associated with the values we adopt for our organizations.

As the symptoms proliferate, the politics of the organization increasingly influence decision processes and nearly every individual decision. Processes are put in place to foster involvement, but they just slow things down and result in endless meetings. Speed is impossible. Change is fought. Nothing is as easy to accomplish as it once was. A decline in performance ultimately follows if the symptoms are not addressed. They require immediate attention if culture creep is to be avoided.

Xerox's erstwhile CEO, Ursula Burns, detected symptoms of culture creep when she assumed her job. They included what she called "terminal niceness." She acted fast. In a presentation to her management team, she said, "We know what we do." She described meetings where some people present and others just listen. "And then the meeting ends, and we leave and go, 'Man, that wasn't true.' I'm like, 'Why didn't you say that in the meeting?'" She went on, "Maybe the Xerox family should act a bit more like a *real* family. . . . I want us to stay civil and kind, but we have to be frank—and the reason we can be frank is because we are all in the same family."[4] Nipping culture creep in the bud enabled Burns to turn around the company's culture and help sustain its performance.

UNDERLYING CAUSES OF STAGNATING CULTURES

Beyond a failure to address symptoms immediately, other underlying causes of deteriorating cultures include (1) frequent leadership turnover, especially if it involves bringing in talent from outside the organization unfamiliar with the culture; (2) frequent reorganization that often leads to politicization and other unproductive behaviors; (3) a loss of contact between the top and lower levels of management, usually due to poor communication and inattention on the part of leadership; (4) the introduction of policies and incentives that encourage the abandonment of shared values and behaviors; (5) rapid growth that requires substantial hiring and runs the risk of inadequate screening and training; and (6) slow or no growth that produces a kind of protective mentality.

At the risk of repetition, there is one more cause—success itself. Coors Brewing, IBM, and Volkswagen all enjoyed much success before the rotting of their cultures. Unfortunately, prolonged success is often the greatest enemy of effective cultures.

Arrogance replaces pride. Concern for others, particularly customers, is replaced by concern for self. The growth fostered by success brings many new employees who aren't sufficiently schooled in "how and why we do things around here." Those that try to change the way things are done are rejected. Ideas from outside the organization are ignored. How such symptoms and causes are dealt with determines whether they will proliferate.

LEARN FROM THE MISTAKES OF OTHERS

The reasons so many efforts to reshape cultures fail include the length of the culture change process itself, exaggerated expectations regarding results and timing, other priorities, a loss of momentum often triggered by a loss of top management interest in a process whose progress is often poorly measured, too much emphasis on process vs. results, and failure to follow through with difficult everyday decisions that culture change requires. A list of common causes of failure is shown in box 7.1.

BOX 7.1 Common Reasons Why Culture Change Efforts Fail

1. Leaders fail to establish a rationale and maintain a sense of urgency for change.
2. Culture change is perceived as a top-down process with little participation from the ranks.
3. Leaders delegate the responsibility for change.
4. There is a failure on the part of leaders to identify non-believers and either neutralize them or disengage from them entirely.
5. There is a tendency on the part of top management to vastly overestimate the degree to which it is communicating throughout the organization (both listening and informing).
6. Leaders are not able to lead by the agreed-upon values and behaviors.
7. There is a failure to recognize or act on violations of the newly agreed-upon code of behavior.
8. Leadership turnover encourages members of the organization to wait out the change process until it goes away.
9. Expectations for the magnitude of change and how fast it will happen are just too high.
10. Success is defined and planned as an all-or-nothing event rather than a series of more modest achievements.

LEAD THE CHANGE WITH A PASSION

It may take a dramatic event to call attention to the need for culture change. In the case of Microsoft in 2014, there was no dramatic event. Instead it required an outsider with substantial inside experience to sense that change was needed. But that's not enough. It also required someone with a passion for change. That person was Satya Nadella, someone with twenty years of experience with Microsoft, a perspective shaped by a childhood in India, and significant personal real-world challenges outside the company that enabled him to sense a "loss of soul" in a hard-driving, engineering-oriented software company.[5] Nadella's experience in changing Microsoft's culture is instructive, as we will see.

Leading any kind of change is difficult. But that has often been referred to as the most important, perhaps the defining, task of leadership. According to John Kotter, a leading student of the subject, leaders establish direction, align people, and motivate and inspire, while managers plan and budget, organize and staff, and monitor results vs. plan (control) while "meeting the numbers" and solving problems.[6] Both leaders and managers are important. But note the extent to which the leader's role is closely related to the task of shaping culture. That's the task that Nadella faced in perhaps the world's most famous and iconic high-tech company.

PUT TOGETHER AN ACTION-BASED REGIMEN FOR CHANGE

Have you ever participated in an exercise to examine an organization's mission, values, and accepted ways of doing things in an effort to define or reshape its culture? It's an intellectual exercise that never fails to engage and energize top executives. It allows them to put aside the decisions of the day and engage in creative thought about the values and behaviors that will help them achieve the organization's ultimate goals. People come out of those meetings in a self-congratulatory mood as if they've just done something both interesting and important. Interesting? Yes. Important? Not so fast.

As part of the meeting, a long-term plan of action is mapped out, responsibilities are assigned, and the most immediate deadlines are agreed upon. But then what happens? Some of the responsibilities are carried out and a deadline or two may be met. But the process appears to be long and rigorous. The payoff is somewhat vague and not expressed in financial terms. The energy and enthusiasm of the early meeting(s) are lost in a welter of pressing issues that have to be dealt with before executives can return to the task they vowed to complete—reshaping the culture. Addressing those issues may even necessitate actions that are counter to the behaviors implied by the values. Somehow, there is a drift in leadership attention toward the immediate and important; culture is important, but it can be addressed another day. Like climate change, it can put you out of business, but not in the short run.

In one sense, the task of reshaping and sustaining a culture never ends. But when it comes to culture change, organizations suffer from attention deficit disorder. As a result, basic efforts to lead substantial change and put in motion the changes in culture to be sustained over time have to be completed in a reasonable time frame, often no longer than twelve months.

There is no one formula for reshaping an organization's culture. But experience has suggested that change rarely occurs without most or all of the following actions.

The sequence is not fixed, although there tends to be a flow of actions and responses. They don't necessarily have to occur with precise sequencing. They overlap; some can be carried out in parallel, as the map in figure 7.1 suggests. At the core of a successful effort are three things: communication, measurement, and responsive action. If you like, use the actions described next as a checklist; evaluate yourself and your team on each of them, and act accordingly. Together, they provide a recipe for building the case for change, drawing up the new culture charter, ensuring momentum, and establishing a mindset for the long term.

GET STARTED

Action One: Recognize the Problem. Like the twelve-step regimen for Alcoholics Anonymous, the first step in changing a culture is recognizing the problem. It's leadership's role to recognize the need for change even if others don't. It's the first step in a process that will require time, patience, and perseverance—elements often in short supply.

Sometimes the need for a change in culture goes hand in hand with a change in strategy. Just as they may feed on each other as part of a "performance doom loop," they can also positively reinforce each other if changed simultaneously.[7] But there are other situations in which a culture change is precisely what is needed. What are the signs to look for? Included among them are measures that can be tracked over time, including those of the kind listed earlier. Performance inputs include employee ratings of their workplace, employee trust of their managers

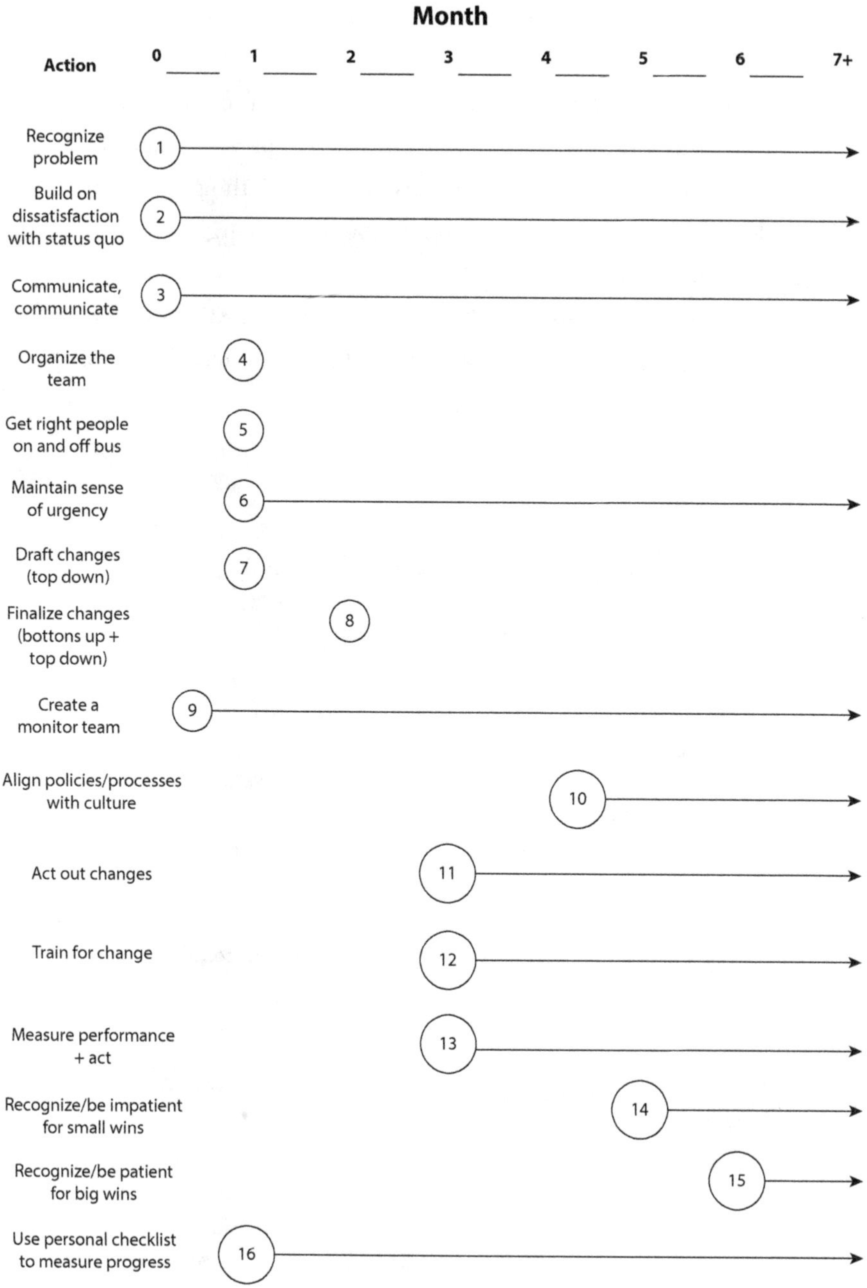

FIGURE 7.1 A culture change map

and peers, employee and customer engagement and retention, time spent in meetings, and management follow-through on commitments. Performance results include such things as safety levels, trends in the rate of innovation, costs, margins, profits, and market share.

Other symptoms to look for are listed in box 7.2. As CEO, you may not have to look hard to find the symptoms. Typically,

---

BOX 7.2 Symptoms Associated With a Dysfunctional Culture

1. A poor sense of mission, shared values, and accepted behaviors on the part of leaders at all levels of the organization
2. New hires with attitudes and motives that don't fit with the culture
3. A tendency to introduce processes, incentives, and controls at odds with the culture
4. Constant planning and replanning
5. The unwillingness or inability of leaders to make commitments and meet them
6. Excessive meetings and bureaucratic activity that impede action; inability to make timely decisions
7. Frequent reorganization
8. Frequent leadership turnover
9. Deteriorating quantitative measures such as employee and customer engagement and retention
10. At the extreme, illegal behavior
11. Deteriorating trends in financial measures

---

they become frequent topics of discussion around the office if you have the will and ability to listen.

In assessing symptoms, it's important to become familiar with the shadow culture—the one that few people talk about, but the one that often drives behavior. One way of doing this, particularly for a new leader, is suggested by Eric Schmidt, who came from another organization to take over as CEO at Google. As he puts it, "Find the smart people first. And to find the smart people, find one of them."[8]

Action Two: Build or Capitalize on Dissatisfaction With the Status Quo. Is the organization ready for change? Do key executives realize the need for change? If so, the probability of success in the change effort is enhanced. If, on the other hand, senior members of the organization are comfortable with the status quo, Michael Beer argues that dissatisfaction with the status quo has to be encouraged.[9]

It doesn't take bankruptcy to make the case for change. Microsoft in 2014 has been described by Satya Nadella as a company whose employees knew it was sick. Personal computer sales were slow. There was disappointing interest in Windows 8, its latest software introduction. Microsoft had missed out on the boom in smartphone sales. The average growth rate in revenues from 2000 to 2014 was 3 percent per year and only 2 percent per year for profits. As Nadella put it, "Most employees didn't think we were headed in the right direction and questioned our ability to innovate. . . . They were fed up with losing. . . . Many felt the company was losing its soul."[10] All of this made his task of leading a change in culture easier. But he had to be sufficiently plugged in to the organization at all levels to be able to know this *and say this* with confidence and without fear of being contradicted by his two well-known and well-respected predecessors, Bill Gates and Steve Ballmer.

Where there is little sense of the need for change, a leader has to make the case for change. Present the numbers comparing the organization's financial performance with that of competitors. If those numbers haven't yet deteriorated, it makes a convincing case for change more difficult to put together. But it can be done with negative trends in leading indicators such as the nonfinancial measures listed above.

Organizations rotting from the inside can still be performing quite well in the public's eye. Performance can be driven by a brilliant strategy or a great product, even as the culture is making decision making and implementation more difficult and slowing the flow of new ideas. For example, Microsoft in 2014—when Nadella became CEO—was still one of the most profitable companies in the world and one that had accumulated a huge hoard of cash. Dissatisfaction with the status quo may not have yet risen to the point where employees were asking for change. Because change is always perceived as difficult, it may be necessary to create dissatisfaction. Here's how some leaders have done it:

1. Document poor performance by making more information available that compares divisions on various financial and nonfinancial measures.
2. Track and share trends in information from leading indicators such as employee engagement and organizational climate surveys.

3. Shut down or sell an underperforming division. Make sure that others in the organization understand why it was done.

4. Begin a process to weed out those identified as poor leaders. If necessary, make it generally known why several of the departing executives left.

Action Three: Communicate, Communicate, Communicate. This is a constant throughout the culture reshaping process and beyond. Start early. Typically leaders wildly overestimate the effectiveness of their communications. Too often, they equate frequent with effective communication. They don't know whether the message has been received because they don't listen for verification. There is a reason why military radio communication requires a "Roger" at the end. It signifies that the message was received. What's your equivalent?

We're not necessarily talking about transparency here. That concerns what is acceptable to communicate. The concern here is effectiveness in whatever is being communicated.

Employees regularly rate the effectiveness of management communication lower than do their leaders—not by a little but by a lot. The result is often confusion and suspicion that the message being received is not accurate. In the absence of effective communication, imagination takes over; small issues become larger.

Look at it this way. Whether you communicate or not, a message will be sent. If it isn't yours, it's likely to be negative.

The message is clear: When in doubt, communicate. Keep it simple and clear. Confirm receipt of the message. Then listen, and do it again. And keep doing it.

Action Four: Organize the Team for Top-Down, Bottom-Up Participation. How do you involve large numbers of people in reshaping a culture without losing control of the process? One answer is to organize a core team to draft a set of values and behaviors that can serve as the basis for obtaining input from the rest of the organization. This team will be responsible as well for ensuring that deadlines are met and momentum is maintained.

In organizing a core team, the natural tendency is to assemble the most senior executives in the organization. That may not be the most sensible course of action. For example, other candidates may include several managers one or two levels down in the organization who will play an important role in implementing whatever is decided upon, individuals who are especially tuned in to the behaviors that have yielded past successes on important initiatives—or one or two iconoclasts who can keep the core team honest when enthusiasm overwhelms reason.

Action Five: Get the Right People on and the Wrong People off the Bus. Ken Kesey, the leader of the Merry Pranksters, an LSD-fueled cult in the 1960s, was famous for a wildly decorated bus in which he transported his followers. He admonished his followers that, "There are going to be times when we can't wait for somebody. Now, you're either on the bus or off the bus."[11] Jim Collins, in researching companies that had achieved greatness after a period of mediocre performance, put it this way: "First who . . . then what." Picking up on Kesey's comment, he went on to say, "The executives who ignited the transformation from good to great . . . first got the right people on the bus [*and in the right seats*] (and the wrong people off the bus) and then figured out where to drive it."[12] The leadership team may include one or two people who are lukewarm supporters of change. This represents an opportunity to either convert them or disengage them from the process early so that they don't prove to be obstructers later on. Some leaders use the initial culture change meetings as an opportunity to identify nonbelievers in the need for change. The leaders then act quickly to ensure that the nonbelievers do not have major responsibilities in the change process. For some nonbelievers, it may be a career-defining moment.

At Microsoft, Nadella made it a high priority to get the right people on the bus even if it meant departures from the senior leadership team. As Nadella described it, "We needed a senior leadership team (SLT) that would lean into each other's problems, promote dialogue, and be effective. We needed everyone to view the SLT as his or her first team, not just another meeting they attended. We needed to be aligned on mission, strategy, and culture."[13]

Action Six: Create and Maintain a Sense of Urgency. The first item in box 7.1, "Common Reasons Why Culture Change Efforts Fail," is most important of all. The pace of competition in today's world doesn't allow for even a year-long front-burner change initiative. There are too many other demands on the time and attention of executives key to the change effort. John Doerr, the highly successful venture capitalist who has also engineered culture change in several high-tech organizations, believes that "time is the enemy of transformation."[14] What's needed is a process designed to be accomplished not only within the tenure of a typical CEO but also within the attention span of a management team.

An organization's culture can be destroyed rapidly. But there is an exaggerated belief about how long it takes to reshape and improve cultures even in large organizations. It requires maintaining a sense of urgency. Frances Frei, who was hired to assist in changing a toxic atmosphere at Uber in 2019, assisted with an assessment of the company's values, beginning with many small group meetings. A subsequent rethinking of the company's values involved all fifteen thousand employees. Their implementation engaged six thousand managers in an extensive retraining exercise designed to give "people tools and concepts to develop quickly as leaders—and, yes, to build more trust" as well as improve their communication skills. She could report, as she wrapped up her full-time participation in the effort, that "Uber was less wobbly. There were still problems to be solved, but indicators such as employee sentiment and brand health were heading in the right direction. . . . Good people were deciding to stay with the company, more good people were joining."[15] How much time did this all take? About nine months.

Tom Ealy, president and CEO of Ameriprise Auto & Home, is from the Frei school of leadership. He believes that "with the right person in the corner office, it's really easy to change culture, and it can happen very quickly. . . . A CEO has an almost magical power to drive normative behavior. . . . [Values] are not the most important part of the culture equation. It's behaviors that matter most to quickly turning the culture tide. . . . In my experience, otherwise fully formed adults can learn and internalize new values in the face of a top leader's consistently inspiring example."[16]

In most cases, the upfront job of changing a culture can be accomplished in six to twelve months. That's roughly the amount of time for intense attention that Satya Nadella allowed himself. When he became the third CEO in Microsoft's history in 2014, he assumed the reigns of a company that was no longer performing like a successful startup or even a company enjoying rapid growth. Its revenues and earnings had begun to flatten out to the point that Microsoft was regarded by many financial analysts as one of the world's most mature tech companies, particularly when compared with its rivals to the south in Silicon Valley. Nadella set forth several things he needed to do "very well right away, during the first year." Among the five things was an effort to "drive cultural change from top to bottom, and get the right team in the right place."[17]

Urgency requires setting tight deadlines with a small amount of allowance for slack in follow-up actions. Make sure the entire process is in place, with appropriate benchmarks, at the outset of the process. One such map for change is shown in figure 7.1.

DRAW UP THE NEW CULTURE CHARTER

Action Seven: Draft Changes in Mission, Values, and Behaviors (Top Down). The primary role of the core team is to draft a set of values and behaviors that can be reviewed by some or all of the other members of the organization for input and suggestions for change. In some cases, a change in mission may be called for as well.

There are many techniques for doing this. Quite often, a facilitator will be brought in to lead the discussion, freeing the

CEO to participate on an equal level with others and providing a voice to others who might be intimidated by a discussion led by the CEO.

A New Mission and Strategy. When Satya Nadella assumed his job as CEO at Microsoft, he detected in his extensive conversations with employees that they sensed some need for change within the organization, but few ideas were being advanced from the ranks. Nadella felt that the company needed "renewal, a renaissance" of its original mission. Under cofounder Bill Gates and then Steve Ballmer, the company's mission had been "a computer on every desk and in every home." But with the emergence of cloud computing, live streaming, and mobile access to the internet, he felt that a product-oriented mission no longer fit the bill. Further, the company's employees needed something about which they and Microsoft's customers could become excited and even passionate. Nadella asked himself what the spirit was "behind the first line of code ever written for the . . . primitive . . . Altair (computer). . . . It was to empower people. And that was still what motivated all of our efforts: *to empower every person and every organization on the planet to achieve more.*"[18] That was something Microsoft employees and observers could get excited about. It was something an organization as important as Microsoft could aspire to achieve.

If the mission were to be achieved, the company would, among other things, have to (1) "reinvent productivity and business processes," especially to empower teams (reflecting the way increasing numbers of people were working); (2) "build the intelligent cloud platform" and open it to other platforms and developers; and (3) migrate users from "needing Windows."

In addition, the company's strategic direction would have to include an emphasis on services for mobile devices as well as the omnipotent Windows orientation inside the company in a world in which the market for computer-based products had matured. It would also require a reshaping of the company's culture.[19]

Nadella avoided most of the mistakes listed in "Common Reasons Why Culture Change Efforts Fail," many of which can be attributed to the fact that the task of reshaping a culture is undertaken so seldom. Let's face it. Your organization will make mistakes in reshaping its culture. However, at least some of the mistakes can be avoided by breaking the task down into the actions shown here. They are based on the successes and failures (learning opportunities) experienced by those heading up organizations large and small.

New Values. "What's the best set of values?" is a question that often arises. It misses the point. The best set is the one that reflects the shared thinking of an organization's leaders (and followers) as well as the assumptions underlying those shared values. A given set of values might appear to be most central to the effectiveness of an organization's culture. But I'll take fit and consistency between values and the shared thinking among members of an organization every time over any particular value. Drew Houston, CEO of Dropbox, an internet services company, illustrates the point well when he says:

> Culture always starts out as the sort of bizarre average of the founders' personalities. But a couple of years ago, we decided to define our values and make our culture explicit. . . .

It seems that most . . . organizations decay as they get older and bigger, and so how do you inoculate your company from the most common things that tend to go wrong?

So we approached it as kind of an engineering problem—what is the opposite of each of those things? We came up with five: Be worthy of trust; sweat the details; aim higher; "we," not "I"; and the fifth is just an image of a smiling cupcake, because we don't want to take ourselves too seriously.[20]

If a smiling cupcake does it for Dropbox, go with it. Research has produced little evidence supporting the argument for any particular value. Jim Collins and Jerry Porras concluded from their landmark study of "visionary" companies "built to last" that "there is no 'right' set of values for being a visionary company. . . . The crucial variable is not the content of a company's ideology, but how deeply it believes its ideology and how consistently it lives, breathes, and expresses it in all that it does."[21]

Agreed. But strong arguments can be made for some values. I always look for one or two values and associated behaviors that are designed to sustain learning, innovation, and agility. Learning is difficult without shared values such as diversity, inclusion, transparency, and an emphasis on teamwork. These are values and behaviors that are either missing among mediocre performers or, as we have seen, have been forgotten in the day-to-day rush of activity. They are values and behaviors that may usefully be included in any effort to reshape an ineffective culture. It's a leader's responsibility to make sure that those are at least considered by the group.

Other values are so broad that they could be included in a list for any organization. For example, the values of honesty or integrity are universal. For these, it is important to concentrate on the behaviors. Why? Any of several values will get you to the same behavior. Here it's the behavior that is most important.

A "from/to" exercise will draw out both values and behaviors. The "froms" describe what got us here; they represent the status quo. The "tos" describe what will get us where we want to go from here.

It can be difficult for a group to discuss frankly the status quo, particularly if it is deemed a significant part of the problem. A good facilitator will draw out the froms. Data from organizational surveys, when coupled with anecdotes from individual experiences, can help here.

The tos are aspirational. These can also be written by the group as a hypothetical magazine article about the organization five years hence. They are uplifting and more pleasant to talk about. They may trigger additional thoughts about the froms. A set of "froms/tos" for Microsoft—drawn from several sources—at the time that Satya Nadella was leading the transformation is shown in box 7.3.

New Behaviors. Behaviors provide guidelines for "how and why we do things around here." They supply the basis for measurement and action. Values typically do not. That's why the identification of shared behaviors is so important. Values may be inspirational while behaviors are measurable and actionable. But remember, as we saw earlier in the Uber example, behaviors can be used to weaponize values against themselves.

BOX 7.3 Examples of "Froms" and "Tos" for Microsoft, 2014

From:	To:
Rigid, closed environment	Open environment
Fixed mindset	Growth mindset
Complainers	Fixers
Confederacy of fiefdoms	One company (diverse and inclusive)
Doing what's comfortable within our organization	Reaching out to do things most important for customers
Prove that you're the smartest in the room (know-it-alls)	Admit that you don't know everything (learn-it-alls)
Accountability = delivering on time and hitting numbers trumps everything	Accountability = meeting customer needs
Formal meetings + hard-to-skip organization levels	Informal meetings + skip organization levels whenever needed
Stack-ranking performance management system: top-good-average-below average-poor, with 10 percent poor ranking required	No stack ranking; instead, a collaboration supported by continual feedback and coaching, with compensation in the hands of managers vs. algorithms

Sources: Herminia Ibarra, Aneeta Rattan, and Anna Johnston, "Satya Nadella at Microsoft: Instilling a Growth Mindset," London Business School case No. CS-18-008, June 2018; Austin Carr and Dina Bass, "The Nadellaissance," *Bloomberg Businessweek*, May 6, 2019; and Satya Nadella, *Hit Refresh: The Quest to Rediscover Microsoft's Soul and Imagine a Better Future for Everyone* (New York: Harper Business, 2017), pp. 100–102.

A from-to exercise provides another opportunity to observe nonbelievers. A CEO acting as a participant rather than a facilitator in the group has an added responsibility and opportunity to identify those who don't believe in the importance of the effort. When it comes time for implementing the reshaping process, it's important not to give these people key roles in the process. In my experience, nonbelievers can sabotage the process either sooner or later. The sooner they are confronted, the less nonproductive effort will be expended in implementing the culture change.

Action Eight: Finalize the Statement (Bottom-Up and Top-Down). Once a set of values and behaviors has been developed by the core team, it is time to involve most or all of the rest of the members of the organization in the process. Involvement is the first step in two-way communication critical to the eventual implementation of change.

Fortunately, today's networking technology has simplified the process of involving everyone. This, for example, is what Sam Palmisano, Lou Gerstner's successor as CEO at IBM, did when he opened up the organization's values for discussion in a 2003 "values jam" conducted over the internet. During a designated period, over 140,000 IBM employees commented on the existing set of values and behaviors. They suggested ideas that led to a reworking of the company's three basic values that were first defined forty years earlier.[22] It was all done in a matter of hours (two seventy-two-hour sessions) vs. the weeks or months required in pre-internet days.

Once the inputs have been considered and either rejected or accepted by the core team, the entire process can be documented, with the results communicated again to everyone in the organization along with information about how the changes will be implemented.

ENSURE MOMENTUM

Action Nine: Create a Monitor Team. Change requires monitoring—tracking progress, making sure deadlines are met, ensuring the quality of the change process, reporting successes and lessons learned, and generally keeping the organization informed. It may later become, as it has in some organizations, the equivalent of a culture committee that can be used as a sounding board for new ideas and initiatives ranging from corporate events to strategic decisions.

A monitor, regardless of what it is called, supports the leadership of the change process without replacing it. It is intended as an additional resource. Its primary concern is change without the distractions of day-to-day management.

Where and what should the team monitor? Too often, leaders neglect to stay in touch with managers in the ranks, especially frontline managers and those to whom they report in middle management. As a result, communication from the bottom to the top often suffers as messages are interpreted or even blocked by managers in the middle. Once it is organized, the monitor team can correct this with frequent measurement of trends in responses to the prompts—such as those shown in box 7.4—along with appropriate follow-up. After the first six months, the frequency can be reduced to six-month and then yearly measurements.

BOX 7.4 Prompts Posed to Frontline and Middle Managers by the Monitor Team

Please rate the degree of your agreement with each of the following statements by noting a number (1 = strongly disagree, 4 = neither disagree nor agree, 7 = strongly agree).

1. I understand the need for changing the culture of this organization.
2. The right people are leading this change.
3. I feel that I have been involved in the culture change process.
4. The new shared values and behaviors we are adopting are the right ones.
5. Whether I agree with the shared values and behaviors toward which we are working, I am enthusiastic about the process we are following to get there.
6. I have been kept well informed throughout the change process to date.
7. What we are doing is important enough to warrant time from my day-to-day management tasks.

Action Ten: Align Measures, Incentives, Policies, and Processes with the Desired Culture. It's a fool's errand to attempt to align culture and strategy at the rate strategies have to change these days in an agile organization. After all, a well-designed culture should be able to support any number of strategies. (Remember figure 1.1?) Instead, focus attention on making sure that values and behaviors are aligned with other policies, processes, and incentives.

What gets measured is what gets managed, especially if appropriate action (recognition or corrective action) follows. In this case, what gets measured are the behaviors that everyone has agreed to. Too often, performance measures aren't linked to the values and behaviors that are supposedly shared by all or most members of the organization. Where that's the case, which do you think takes precedence—some set of vague shared values and behaviors or the measures that may appear on a performance review form—or more importantly, those that are linked to recognition or reward?

We discussed in chapter 5 examples of the care taken by leaders to ensure that policies, incentives, and organization are structured to honor and encourage desired values and behaviors in great places to work. They repeatedly ask the kind of questions that reflect what is important in any culture change effort, questions such as:

1. Are we measuring the right things?
2. Do our policies reinforce the message sent by our new shared values and behaviors?
3. Are we recognizing and rewarding the behaviors we've agreed on not only in our performance appraisals but also in the way we provide advice and feedback?
4. Does the organization reflect the way we want to work? For example, does it facilitate cross-functional coordination (if that is an objective) or encourage work in teams (if that is desired)?
5. Do our policies encourage the kind of communications (top-down, bottom-up, level-skipping) we have said we value?

6. Do practices, such as the way we conduct our meetings, reinforce values (such as frankness) and behaviors (such as constructive debate)?

Action Eleven: Act Out the Changes. This action sounds simple, but it may pose real challenges. Leaders are, by the nature of their roles, on display. They are watched by those around them in the organization. Every move and action is subject to interpretation and judgment. Actions involving people are judged in terms of their fairness to others. Were the right people hired, recognized, promoted, transferred, or fired?

Did the actions and the way they were carried out reflect the organization's values? Did they generally make sense to others? Or were they confusing, raising questions about a leader's motives and the values themselves? Is there a pattern to the actions? Are behaviors not only consistent with the organization's culture but also consistent with one another? Are they doing what is expected? If so, they build trust. If, on the other hand, they produce surprises, they destroy recognized patterns of behavior and trust. No one knows what to expect next.

In the process of changing a culture, consciously crafted actions may be needed. Steve Odland, during the time he served as chairman and CEO of Office Depot, began each management meeting by leading a recitation of the company's missions and values. Akin to an elementary school Pledge of Allegiance, the act might sound corny. But I watched the faces of people in those meetings reciting the mission and values. They were dead serious. Odland's objective was to ingrain in the minds of his senior associates the mission and values statement so strongly that without thinking they would act it out.

Action Twelve: Train for Change. This sounds mundane, but training is the responsibility of managers at every level in the organization. The process again begins at the top. The core team has to decide on the kinds of behaviors that its members will demonstrate—whether it involves mentoring, means of communication, working alongside those on the frontline, and so on. This becomes the basis for the training of managers at lower levels. It may include information about changes in performance measurement to include adherence to the values and behaviors deemed important. The most common process for carrying this out is through some kind of cascading in which managers at each level are responsible for the training of those at the next level. To ensure that the message is not distorted as it travels through the organization, a facilitator can once again be engaged. This also might include members of the monitor team (discussed earlier) from time to time.

Here the importance of high-performing local cultures in the organization should be recognized. Individual leaders may have fostered ways of getting things done that don't always conform with the generally accepted practice. While it may be tempting not to disrupt the status quo, it's important to recognize that such cultures often rely on the skills of an individual leader who may not be in that job forever. This argues for putting in place plans to foster a shift from one set of values and behaviors to the more widely accepted version, recognizing that some elements of the culture (especially artifacts such as the Friday pizza party) may remain unique to local work units.

Now comes the hard part. Too often, the importance of acting out change is lost on those in the organization who should be setting an example for the rest. This has become especially important at a time when inappropriate workplace behavior has become a major issue. What's to be done when a subordinate sees their boss violating a shared value through inappropriate behavior? Do they have enough safety to remind their boss at the appropriate time that the situation might have been handled differently? And has the boss been prepared for such a possibility—perhaps using a previous agreement on acceptable behaviors—so that she or he regards it as a learning moment rather than an act of insubordination? This story can only have a happy ending if the kind of common understanding that Amy Edmondson referred to as "psychological safety" in chapter 4 has been established.[23]

Action Thirteen: Measure Performance and Respond. Once a new set of values and behaviors is identified with a reshaped culture, it's important to make sure they are reflected in both the informal and formal performance measurement systems. Put it to use immediately and daily in on-the-job training and feedback activities. The more formal performance appraisal, if it is used, has to be revised as well to reflect the changes. Ironically, the performance appraisal systems in most of the organizations I have observed at close range don't reflect the values and behaviors they are supposed to be practicing. This chief failing is one of the first things to be corrected as part of the culture change process.

Measurement can cause a real dilemma when it comes to action. What do you do with leaders whose units are making their numbers but, according to results from 360-degree personnel feedback, aren't managing by the agreed-upon values and behaviors? Too many companies simply reward and recognize them, ignoring the fact that they may be damaging the culture. The long-term price to the organization may not be worth the short-term benefits. Others willing to address the problem regard this as a cause for retraining or counseling before firing those who just can't change their behaviors at midcareer. There is a saying that, "If you have to change a manager, often you have to change a manager." The benefits to the organization's culture, its productivity, and its profit performance often leave leaders wondering why they didn't act sooner.

ESTABLISH A MINDSET FOR LONG-TERM CHANGE

Action Fourteen: Recognize, Reward, and Be Impatient for Small Wins. Too often in an effort to reshape culture, success is defined and planned as an all-or-nothing event rather than a series of more modest achievements. That's why it's important to identify some wins that can be achieved in a relatively short period. These may include such things as improvements in quarter-to-quarter employee retention rates, higher levels of trust between employees and their leaders, or better numbers for such things as plans to stay in the organization. When achieved, the wins are celebrated without too much fanfare. Then it's time to get back to work on the next win.

Action Fifteen: Be Patient for Big Wins. The big wins are those that have a major impact on profits and growth. They result from several smaller wins. For example, we know from the research mentioned earlier that in organizations with high levels of contact between employees and customers, trends in employee satisfaction, engagement, commitment, and loyalty are reflected in the same kinds of behavior in customers. If gradual in coming, the economic impact of these customer behaviors can be dramatic. But it takes time—perhaps a year or two. And it requires patience. When it happens—and it will—it provides an opportunity to reinforce the change process by reminding everyone on the bus why they undertook the journey in the first place. It also provides an opportunity to remind everyone that the journey is never-ending. It will continue to require diligence even though many of the behaviors that triggered the change will have become a habit or at least above question—just part of "how and why we do things around here."

Action Sixteen: Use a Personal Leadership Reminder List to Measure How Things Are Going. The actions described above provide the basis for a personal reminder list that can be used periodically—and soon after the start of the process—as a way of evaluating its success. The reminder list is shown in box 7.5.

BOX 7.5 The Culture Change Reminder List*

1. My organization understands why we're doing this.
2. We are capitalizing sufficiently on dissatisfaction in the organization with the status quo.
3. The organization generally gives this effort a high priority.
4. Our communication regarding the change process— sending, confirming receipt, and listening—is sufficiently

---

frequent and effective. (Little is being left to rumor and misinterpretation in the organization.)

5. Teams are organized well for both top-down and bottom-up participation.

6. Nonbelievers in the process have been removed from positions of responsibility for implementing it.

7. We are maintaining a sense of urgency and meeting our deadlines.

8. The new mission statement, underlying assumptions, shared values, and accepted behaviors reflect the work and inputs of people at all levels in the organization.

9. We have a monitor team to track the effort, provide support to leaders primarily responsible for the change, and ensure that other actions by leaders do not compromise progress to change the culture.

10. Measures, incentives, policies, and processes are being aligned with elements of the desired culture.

11. Leaders at all levels are acting out the changes in values and behaviors that were agreed upon.

12. There is sufficient training for change.

13. Measures have been put in place to track progress in behavior change.

14. Those unable to adapt to new ways of thinking about "how and why we do things around here" are being retrained or counseled out of the organization.

15. Small wins have been identified and are being recognized and celebrated.

16. Leaders are realistic about the amount of time it will take for big wins.

*Rate yourself and your organization from 1 (do not agree) to 7 (agree completely) on each statement. Do it periodically—at first every two months during the first year. Give 1s and 2s a red label, 3s through 5s a yellow label, and 6s and 7s a green label. Compare your profile with the one prepared by the monitor team. Working with that team, develop a plan of action to achieve a green for each statement.

Earlier, I stressed the need to maintain a sense of urgency and to confine the concentrated change effort to as little as six months before other management priorities begin to crowd out the initial enthusiasm for the change. What I have in mind is diagrammed in figure 7.1. The sixteen actions outlined there are positioned across a timeline for six months of concentrated effort followed by a much longer harvesting time. Conscious efforts to change during the first six months become leader habits later on, reinforced as organization morale improves and the effects of the change begin to show up in improved financial performance. This is what has happened at Microsoft.

Satya Nadella's tenure as CEO at Microsoft has produced remarkable change and success. The company's value has more than doubled, at times crossing the $1 trillion mark to become the most valuable in the world. Its cloud-based service business has grown from a relatively small business to more than 200 million subscribers. Nadella himself refuses to celebrate such accomplishments. As he says, "At Microsoft we have this very bad habit of not being able to push ourselves because we just feel very self-satisfied with the success we've had. . . . We're learning how not to look at the past."[24]

Most will credit the success to a change in strategic direction, the effort to give cloud-based services (Azure) at least as much attention in the company's business mix as Windows software. After all, revenue and profit numbers don't lie. But they may not tell the whole story either. Some at Microsoft "attribute its reemergence as a tech power to a sort of cultural rehab, involving what Nadella calls corporate 'empathy.'"[25]

Not that the task is ever finished. Employees, both current and departed, say that "while the culture has improved, the company still struggles with the same old political infighting and ugly employee behavior."[26]

Leaders play an important role in culture change. But few played a more central role than Pete Coors when he vowed to change the culture of Coors Brewing described at the outset of this chapter. In an organization with a command-and-control management tradition, it would have to begin with the CEO. First, Coors initiated steps to have the problem of the beer can's design addressed. Then he began several other important initiatives. One was to encourage everyone to think more broadly about quality—not only in terms of the beer itself but also in terms of the overall customer experience, including packaging and the kinds of associations that the Coors beer-drinking experience might bring to the minds of potential consumers. The mission, as he outlined it, became one not only of making the best beer on the market but also of delivering the best beer-drinking experience.

But Pete Coors didn't stop there. He concluded that the company's senior executives could benefit from a refresher course on continuous quality improvement; it would tie into efforts to change the culture. To give that effort added credibility, he decided to take responsibility for the course, even leading some of the classes. He made sure that the course placed appropriate emphasis on the need to spend time in the marketplace to find out what potential customers wanted and to spend time out in the industry—not only to benchmark Coors against its competitors but also to pick up ideas that might be brought back to

Golden, Colorado. No longer would the company operate with its wagons circled.

These were just some of the things that Pete Coors started. He took steps to end the conflict resolution process that had led to the hospital emergency room. And most importantly, he initiated a series of discussions about the kind of place Coors should be in which to work and what needed to be done to get there.

In all likelihood, Pete Coors saved the company from the new sources of competition that it was about to face. Coors today operates successfully as a company merged with another brewer, Molson Coors. Coors' practice of employing stories such as this one—I'm sure I wasn't the first to hear it—is typical of other leaders of organizations characterized by long histories of culture-centered success.

Coors' accomplishment deserves all the more attention because of the strength, not the weakness, of his organization's culture. It takes less effort and imagination to reshape a weak culture. Values, behaviors, practices, and policies die hard, especially in organizations where employees remember when they worked well. Fortunately, Peter Coors had the determination and the credibility to reshape a very strong culture.

There is a growing interest today in culture markers—those things to look for in an organization's culture that suggest its future performance. We considered a number of them earlier. But the most important marker of all is the organization's leader, her passion for the mission, and his belief in the importance of pursuing it through the vehicle of a great workplace peopled by those driven to learn and innovate. It's the leader's role to sense the need for change and to see that it happens, to set an example for the rest of the organization, and to inspire a passion for the organization's mission, values, and behaviors. This takes many personal qualities. Jim Collins identified perhaps the two most important—personal humility and professional will—in a landmark study of companies spurred to new heights. When applied to the task of creating and maintaining a competitive culture, these qualities lie behind several other essential leader behaviors. I'll have more to say about this next.

IF YOU REMEMBER NOTHING ELSE . . .

- Responsibility for leading a culture change can't be delegated by the CEO.
- Establish a rationale (such as dissatisfaction with the status quo) and a sense of urgency for the change.
- Invite participation in the change from the ranks after providing some guidance from the top.
- Quickly identify and excuse nonbelievers from the task; disengage from those unable to act out newly agreed-upon values and behaviors.
- Communicate more than you think is necessary.
- Measure and celebrate success as a series of modest achievements.
- Be patient for significant long-term wins and impatient for smaller short-term wins.
- Follow a plan for achieving significant change in six to twelve months, a period during which it is feasible to maintain momentum.

Chapter Eight

LEAD FOR COMPETITIVE ADVANTAGE
THROUGH CULTURE

THERE IS little point in trying to create and maintain a competitive culture without a leader's belief, enthusiasm, and passion. One problem is that the task is unlike all others confronting a leader. It's not one of the thirty daily fifteen-minute tasks, meetings, or decisions to be made and put aside by a CEO. It's not the bright idea that commands a CEO's attention for a week or so. It's not even the execution of a major strategic plan. As Lou Gerstner, former chairman and CEO of IBM says, "If the CEO isn't living and preaching the culture and isn't doing it consistently, then it just doesn't happen."[1]

Management literature is often criticized for creating a cult of the CEO—giving the CEO too much credit for the success or failure of an organization or a particular strategy. It is hard, however, to overstate the impact of a leader, whether CEO or group manager, on an organization's culture. A culture is, after all, about people and their behaviors, interactions leading to performance. A leader variously plays the roles of instigator, conscience, and cheerleader in the process of reshaping the mission and culture of an organization.

Let's face it. Leaders have many other things to think about and act on than culture, from day-to-day firefighting to performance against goals. These tasks are often highly visible, represented by numbers, and given high short-term priority.

It may take a dramatic event to call attention to the need for culture change. In the case of Microsoft, there was no dramatic event. It required an outsider with substantial inside experience to sense that change was needed. But that was not enough. It also required someone with a passion for change. That person was Satya Nadella, who stresses the importance of the task this way:

> I like to think that the C in CEO stands for culture. The CEO is the curator of an organization's culture. . . . Anything is possible for a company when its culture is about listening, learning, and harnessing individual passions and talents to the company's mission. Creating that kind of culture is my chief job as CEO.[2]

It requires a certain passion to lead and sustain a culture change, one that can emerge in many ways.

When John Legere surprised even himself by signing on to turn around a lagging T-Mobile wireless carrier, he had a kind of epiphany. He says, "I (didn't) need to fight my way up the hierarchy anymore," worrying about his suits and hair. He grew his hair long and began dressing in bright magenta (the company color) T-Mobile T-shirts and accessories. This could be his laboratory, his experiment of a lifetime. He marshaled his years of experience in the industry and the knowledge that his larger, more complacent competitors were able to survive due to regulatory protection. They persisted despite lacking the drive to put employees and customers first. So he threw himself into the job. He decided to "become the brand" as part of the effort to remake the culture and create a great place to work, one capable of taking on the Goliaths of the industry. To remind himself every day of the importance of the task of reshaping a culture (alongside that of leading strategic changes), he said, "Seven days a week, 24 hours a day, I wear T-Mobile gear."[3] While that might be a bit extreme for some, it illustrates the nature of the sustained leadership passion required to compete through culture.

In his study of companies going from "good to great," Jim Collins put his finger on the kind of leader that could take them on that journey. As mentioned in chapter 7, he characterized it as level 5 leadership and defined it as "a paradoxical blend of personal humility (a compelling modesty) and professional will (unwavering resolve . . . to do what must be done)."[4]

While leaders associated with positive performance in this book may fall across a range on the modesty scale, they share a professional will characterized by their willingness to put their organizations before themselves. This combination provides an umbrella over several more detailed things that leaders know and do to enable their organizations to perform leadership job

---

BOX 8.1 Leader Culture Roadmap

Observations of leaders who have done it well provide a roadmap for leading a culture:

1. Keep it simple. Values? Three or four will do; after all, IBM has been served well by no more than that over nearly a century. That number is easy to remember.

2. Keep behaviors—"why and how we do things around here"—simple and also memorable.

3. Exhibit the values and behaviors yourself. Be visible. Communicate face-to-face with the front line.

4. Hire for attitude (belief in mission, values, and behaviors), train well, provide great support systems, and leave the rest up to the good judgment of associates.

5. Measure. Make sure it's fair, understandable, and, when useful, public. Maintain a balanced scorecard of over-all measures that *predict* the future performance of the organization.

6. Take corrective action based on measurement and done in ways intended to send messages to the rest of the organization. Above all, act in a timely fashion on staffing mistakes, including those who make their numbers but can't manage by the culture's shared values and behaviors. Remember Jim Collins's admonition to get the right people on and off the bus.

number one—compete through culture. Box 8.1 lists some of the more important elements of that wisdom.

We can put some meat on these bones by focusing on leader behaviors that have proven important in building and preserving effective cultures over the years.

LIVE THE CULTURE: PROVIDE A ROLE MODEL

A leader's actions and behaviors matter a great deal. Someone who does this well may foster the same behavior in those being led. Research at McKinsey & Co. has found that "transformations are 5.3 times more likely to succeed when leaders model the behavior they want employees to adopt."[5]

Calculated behaviors are just as important as those that come naturally. With the latter, we are often unaware of the signals our behaviors send, whether for better or worse. That's why executive coaching has become so popular; it may take an objective observer to make us aware of them.

In contrast, we're conscious of calculated behaviors and the messages they are intended to send. The best meet certain criteria:

1. Do they contribute positively to business performance?
2. Do they help people develop themselves?
3. Do they send signals about leadership attitudes and skills that help improve personal relationships and performance?
4. Are they easily observable?
5. Are they easy to emulate?
6. Will they help maintain a winning culture or change a losing one?

Providing a role model is a philosophy that is being followed by the current generation of leaders. According to one account, "This is a common refrain you hear in Silicon Valley;

the CEO who picks up the stack of newspapers outside the front door, the founder who wipes the counters. With these actions, the leaders demonstrate . . . we're all in this together and none of us are above the menial tasks that need to get done. Mostly, though, they do it because they care so much about the company. Leadership requires passion. If you don't have it, get out now."[6]

Bill Marriott has always thought and acted like an owner. He wanted his employees to do the same. Whenever he picked up a piece of trash, it was a winning move on several fronts. If possible, he did it in front of other Marriott managers. It's easily observable and easy to emulate. Every time it happens, employees who observe it get the message: take responsibility; act like an owner. The message travels fast through the organization. Others have shared the practice. For example, John Wooden, the legendary coach of the UCLA basketball team is said to have picked up trash in the team's locker room. Wooden may have picked up the practice from Ray Kroc, founder of McDonald's, who was known for doing the same outside his company's stores.

When Lou Gerstner became CEO of IBM, he made a telling discovery. His predecessors had over time begun making little or no effort to participate in the company's annual global sales meetings. This in a company known as one of the great sales organizations of the twentieth century. So when he made a conscious decision to attend his first global sales meeting, participate in the discussion, and stay until the end, he not only reminded everyone of the importance of sales to IBM but also underlined the importance of getting priorities right and digging deeply into important activities. It gave a morale boost to a portion of the organization that was feeling underappreciated. It communicated not constancy but change—the idea that things would be different from the past at IBM.

To change the strategic mindset of his leadership team at Microsoft, Satya Nadella took several calculated actions. He divided the Windows division into two teams, Azure (cloud-based services) and Office (software). He stopped making frequent use of the word *windows* in his communications. And, according to a former Microsoft executive, "He just started omitting 'Windows' from sentences. . . . Suddenly everything from Satya was 'cloud, cloud, cloud.' "[7]

Some might object to calculated behaviors as being too manipulative, especially when compared to natural behaviors of which we may be largely unconscious. But who knows? Kroc, Wooden, and Marriott may just have been neat freaks. Both calculated and natural behaviors contribute to an effective package that leaders display. The fact that calculated behaviors are more controllable makes them important tools in the leadership toolkit. They are most effective when they are repeated—repetition leads to replication—with little or no fanfare.

ENSURE FAIRNESS

Whether or not it is one of the shared core values of the organization, fairness comes up time and again in surveys as something employees value very highly. We know from research that a leader's fairness in the eyes of her employees is often assessed in terms of the most visible actions that a leader takes: recognizing, hiring, and firing the "right people."[8] Every time a leader makes one of these decisions, the quality of the decision is judged by a jury of several peers. Over time, it adds up to a judgment of whether a leader is fair or not. Fairness affects credibility, trust, and an employee's willingness to follow his leader.

Fairness is in the eye of the beholder. It is relative, not absolute. This is why it is advisable to err on the side of fairness and measure their judgments periodically in dealings with employees.

PRACTICE SOME FORM OF SERVANT LEADERSHIP

Effective cultures are often led by people who practice servant leadership. In the U.S. Marines, for example, it is a long-standing practice that enlisted personnel eat before the officers.

A notion popularized by Robert Greenleaf in 1970, servant leadership in its purest form is considered "making one's main priority to serve rather than to lead."[9] It became a guiding philosophy for organizations such as ServiceMaster and furniture manufacturer Herman Miller. Broadly speaking, it is about serving those reporting to you by giving them latitude to do their jobs, helping them develop their skills, and then opening doors for them in the rest of the organization.

Servant leadership can take many forms, planned or spontaneous. The former was the practice in the ServiceMaster organization to organize regular events in which managers served beverages and food to the frontline employees who performed cleaning, catering, and other services offered by the company.

I observed the latter as a guest at a ServiceMaster board meeting. Bill Pollard, the company's CEO at the time, spilled a cup of coffee on the rug in the board room during a break in the meeting. He didn't ask someone to clean it up. Instead, he asked someone to get him a specific cleaning fluid from the kitchen, whereupon he proceeded to clean up the spot himself in front of some of his board members. He did it without hesitation. No one offered to help. Board members seemed not to pay much attention to their CEO hard at work on his hands and knees.

Perhaps the best measure of servant leadership is the amount of time leaders spend helping their subordinates achieve their goals, often through coaching that can be implicit or explicit. Bill Campbell, at one time a football coach at Columbia, became a legendary coach and mentor to the leaders of many of Silicon Valley's most successful companies. One widely read work about his coaching philosophy sums up the importance of the activity this way: "The higher you climb, the more your success depends on making other people successful. By definition, that's what coaches do. . . . Whereas mentors dole out words of wisdom, coaches roll up their sleeves and get their hands dirty. . . . They take responsibility for making us better without taking credit for our accomplishments."[10]

SERVE AS CHEERLEADER AND CONSCIENCE

A leader variously plays the roles of instigator, conscience, and cheerleader in the process of reshaping and maintaining the mission and culture of an organization. For example,

Southwest Airlines began as an underdog in the airline industry. With its low-cost, low-fare strategy employing nontraditional approaches to air travel and a brand centered around love (actually luv), high-energy personnel, and a fun flying experience, it posed a threat to the status quo. Competitors tried to put it out of business. But it survived. Veterans of those early days constantly reminded Employees and Customers (always capitalized) of the company's plucky, underdog position. Its employees had to try harder to be better. No one communicated this more ardently or more frequently than CEO Herb Kelleher, who made sure that his public behavior made him the company's biggest cheerleader. (He didn't have to act; he was like that when no one was looking.)

The strategy, driven by a unique competitive culture, worked. It worked so well that Southwest would, of course, become one of the industry leaders, literally the largest low-fare airline in the world (with a New York Stock Exchange listing of LUV). The dog chasing the auto caught it. Now what?

The challenge was to make sure that this proud organization didn't become arrogant. Kelleher shifted the emphasis from that of an underdog to an organization seeking to maintain a "pioneering spirit." It was a never-ending quest and one of which employees had to be reminded often. In the process, Kelleher had transitioned from the role of cheerleader to that of conscience of the organization with the primary task of demonstrating the pioneering spirit necessary to continue a focus on people, both Employees and Customers. It was a role he handed off to CEO Gary Kelly, who until his recent retirement pulled off the equally daunting task of maintaining the spirit.

MAINTAIN HIGH LEADERSHIP VISIBILITY

The McKinsey study cited earlier also concluded that "nearly 50 percent of employees cite the CEO's visible engagement and commitment to transformation as the most effective action for engaging frontline employees."[11] Good leaders inherently understand this, even if—or especially because—it makes them look human in the eyes of those working at the lowest levels in the organization.

A large U.S. concierge service organization with hospitals and hotels as its customers, Towne Park, encourages its leaders to spend a lot of time in the field. Some of the time is spent with clients and in business development work. But all of its senior managers are required to spend two days every month—"wheels down and sleeves up" time—working alongside employees parking cars and providing other services to hotel guests and hospital patients. It sends a strong message that leadership cares about what is going on in the trenches, ensures that top managers are aware of what goes on in the field, and provides a channel of communication from the bottom to the top of the organization. I was told, "Employees love seeing their bosses run, get yelled at by impatient customers, and experience first-hand what they go through." The story about the CEO who backed into a post, smashing an expensive auto, is told and retold even though it happened years ago.[12]

If you followed Walmart only by headlines in the media selectively describing its human resource policies—relatively low wages, limited benefits, alleged gender discrimination—you'd have had to wonder how Walmart was able to have any success maintaining a workforce. And yet, talk to most store employees and they'll tell you that they like their jobs and intend to stay there. One reason is that they are likely to know their boss and their boss's boss. That's because Walmart leaders spend four days a week in the field, much of it working alongside store employees. Starting with the chairman and CEO, leaders engage in a competition in which they select a favorite merchandise item, promote it in the stores (by setting up a product display themselves), and see who can sell the most, sometimes in competition with displays created by store employees. When the employees win, the news travels fast that this is a company in which you can have some fun while working hard. Even though it's the largest nongovernmental employer in the world, Walmart's leaders are still trying to ensure that its employees experience it as the small brainchild of Sam Walton.

By the looks of his small office, John Legere must not have spent much time there when he led T-Mobile. There was barely a place to sit, given the stuffed animals and other T-Mobile paraphernalia that covered much of the space. He says he systematically marked off time for round-robin visits to the company's eighteen major call centers. He even regularly observed his and his competitors' retail store employees changing shifts, noting that competitors' employees changed from company gear to street clothes while T-Mobile employees wore theirs out of the store.[13] We should believe him. It paid off in engaged employees, 96 percent of which were giving him positive ratings on Glassdoor shortly before he completed his management contract and turned the job over to a successor.[14]

LISTEN AND RESPOND

In my experience, most CEOs are not particularly reliable sources of information about the effectiveness of their organizations' cultures. A *WSJ.Insights* survey conducted in March 2016 found that 51 percent of C-suite executives believed that their organization's culture "puts people first." Only 28 percent of the leaders at lower levels of these same organizations believed it.[15] This lack of top management knowledge, often resulting from a leader's failure to maintain effective lines of communication or sufficient contact with operating levels, damages a culture.

Consider what happened at Wells Fargo, whose employees, as we saw in box 5.1 in chapter 5, were found to be defrauding customers under the pressure of hard-to-meet sales goals and incentives. Let's give top management the benefit of the doubt and chalk it up to ignorance of what was going on down in the organization. Ironically, just months before the fraud was disclosed, Tim Sloan, then president and COO and later CEO, is quoted as saying, "People are our competitive advantage, so we care for our team members and want them to enjoy what they're doing. Customers tell us they do business with Wells Fargo because our people care about them—that is our Vision."[16] Clearly, Sloan either was not in touch with what was going on at the bank's operating level or had some reason to overlook it. Whatever the case, Sloan himself was called before a U.S. Congressional committee to face questioning from federal lawmakers representing injured constituents. Under withering questioning, he failed to present a convincing case in defense of the bank and the practices of its leadership. Four days later he resigned from his position.

This doesn't mean that a leader needs to listen and be responsive to every individual need throughout the organization. The leader does, however, need to be observed making the effort to listen and respond to employees at all levels. All it often takes is a personal effort that can be observed by others, especially if this is combined with incentives designed to cascade the practice down into the organization.

Too often, leaders assume that results from the annual employee engagement survey represent evidence that listening is going on. Nothing could be further from the truth. Information in an employee engagement survey can help establish overall trends in important measures across the organization. But listening is an individual, personal, ongoing activity. It requires unique individual responses.

What leaders may hear are the usual levels of complaint that accompany expectations and accountability in a high-performance organization. The best leaders listen for much more serious observations from reliable, loyal members of the organization—for example, that meeting time is eating up analysis and decision time, that people conceal their real feelings about programs of action and then fail to perform after supposedly committing to do so, that leadership is failing to identify and disengage promptly from those unable to manage by the agreed-on shared values. Listening has an important purpose. It is intended to trigger timely action.

None of this matters if there is a disconnect between listening and response. That's often a signal that very little learning and personal development is taking place. That message also travels rapidly down through the ranks if it is occurring at the highest ranks in the organization.

PRACTICE AND ENCOURAGE NO-SURPRISES LEADERSHIP AND TRUST

My research has confirmed the centrality of trust in the process of reshaping a culture. It also suggests that no-surprises leadership is a primary factor in fostering trust, as discussed in chapter 5. It's worth repeating.

For years, we've identified "no surprises" with the notion that you don't surprise your boss. The kind I'm talking about here essentially stands that idea on its head. It means that your boss doesn't surprise you. To practice it, a leader has to understand the expectations of her followers. That requires direct contact with employees, a personal interest in them, and information sharing about mutual expectations for the job to be done. Research has identified an important relationship between met expectations and trust. Trust in leaders is found in great places to work as well as cultures that boost performance. An example from the world of baseball described in box 8.2 illustrates the effectiveness of these dynamics.

Trust among members of an organization yields speed, ability, less bureaucracy and need for follow-up, and a better place to work for the right people. While we are told that it is fostered by transparency, communication, and a willingness to display vulnerability, the dependability represented by no-surprises

BOX 8.2: No-surprises leadership and the 2016 baseball World Series

There is probably no professional sports business where the amount of money invested in talent is a poorer predictor of athletic success than major league baseball. In a sport that is played nearly every day over a six-month season, it can be argued that the effectiveness of a team's chemistry (read culture) is more important than the individual skills of the players. Players have to trust each other and their leader. Developing that trust is an important leadership task. No-surprises leadership is an important factor in building that trust. One has to look no further than the 2016 World Series between the Chicago Cubs and Cleveland Indians for a memorable example.

The president of the Cubs, Theo Epstein, and the manager of the Indians, Terry Francona, worked together to lead the Boston Red Sox to two world championships before departing to manage elsewhere.

Early in his career before a game one day, Epstein learned an important lesson from an unlikely source, Craig Shipley, a veteran utility infielder whose play will otherwise not long be remembered. As Epstein tells it: "He said every player's been lied to by management—or thinks they're about to be lied to by management. . . . That helped the light bulb go off that, yeah, you can get a real advantage just by being honest with your players all the time. . . . You end up building better relationships with players. They start to trust you, and you can ask more out of them when they trust you."[*]

Francona not only shares this belief, but he also practices no-surprises leadership to achieve trust. According to one of his former players: "Every spring training, he opened up with a speech. No. 1, he would say, 'I respect you, and you're never going to play for someone who cares more about you than I do.' And 2, he would say, 'I will not lie to you. A lot of times I'm going to tell you something you don't want to hear. But I'm not going to lie.'"[†]

The fact that Epstein's and Francona's teams faced each other for the World Series championship in 2016 suggests that these practices worked at least for them that year and probably in succeeding years in which their teams continued to have above-average winning records despite payrolls that weren't the highest in baseball.

[*]Tyler Kepner, "Theo Epstein and Terry Francona Have Their Players' Backs," *New York Times*, October 25, 2016, https://www.nytimes.com/2016/10/26/sports/baseball/theo-epstein-and-terry-francona-have-their-players-back.html.
[†]Kepner, "Theo Epstein and Terry Francona."

leadership is important. Leaders who set and either meet expectations or explain why they can't be met engender trust. Trust is like money in the bank when it comes to managing change, including the implementation of a new strategy.

TAKE TIMELY ACTION WITH NONBELIEVERS

Nonbelievers can sabotage any kind of change. When the subject is the organization's culture, it can be particularly devastating. That's why it's important to identify what they are doing and act in a timely way to address the problem.

Tony Hsieh's efforts to introduce the "manager-less" culture of Holocracy at Zappos represented some of the biggest challenges he faced at the online shoe retailer. The goal of eliminating managers from the organization is a daunting one. For decades we have studied the importance of management. We have aspired to occupy management roles. And then Hsieh comes along and tells us that we have to learn not to lead— at least in the traditional sense. The alternative is to leave the organization. Typical of Hsieh's nonconfrontational leadership style were the substantial incentives that Zappos had offered for years to those who decided that the company was not for them and opted out of its orientation program. Similarly, nonbelievers in Holocracy could accept incentives to leave. Those departing early in the transition represented more than 15 percent of all managers.[17] Hsieh didn't ask them to leave; instead, he made it easy to do so. It was critical if this controversial initiative was to have any chance of success.

Leaders too often get hung up on the issue of an individual's indispensability to the organization. In my experience, so-called indispensable people who cannot manage by shared values and exhibit the generally accepted behaviors that go with the values impede progress and performance. As mentioned earlier, when they are let go, the organization often breathes a collective sigh of relief, closes ranks, and raises its performance levels.

RECOGNIZE AND REWARD LEARNING AND TEACHING

Learning and teaching are practices characteristic of an innovative organization able to alter its strategies to meet changing conditions while maintaining a strong and adaptive culture.[18] At the Mayo Clinic, the primary teaching mechanism is "the spirit of collaboration" that characterizes the teams that deliver its health care. One of the organization's principles is "teach, don't blame."[19] Those same physicians who teach may also be studying in the organization's career and leadership program. Innovation at Mayo has served as an example for the rest of the health care industry while producing outstanding outcomes for patients with typically more complex afflictions.

Learning and teaching often lead to evidence-based decision making. It requires a particular mindset among leaders. Evidence is given more value than opinion in decision making. Managers are encouraged to develop and present evidence in support of their arguments. And leaders have to expect to be supplied with evidence that runs counter to their opinions. As Stefan Thomke asks of leaders in learning organizations, "How willing are you to be confronted every day with how wrong you are?"[20]

ENCOURAGE SELFLESS, BOUNDARYLESS LEADERSHIP BEHAVIORS

At Nucor, the high-performing specialty steel operator of minimills, a typical story is about the electricians who, when informed that the electrical grid at the company's Hickman, Arkansas, minimill had failed, made their way to Hickman to help get the facility back up and running. Malcolm McDonald drove in from an Indiana minimill. Les Hart and Bryson Trimble flew in from Nucor's minimill in Hertford County, North Carolina. Together with local electricians, working twenty-hour shifts, they were able to get the mill up and operating in three days vs. the seven days it would have taken without their help. The punch line, according to one account, is that per the company's values, "No supervisor had asked them to make the trip. . . . They went on their own. . . . There wasn't any direct financial incentive for them."[21] What's particularly remarkable about the story is that it's not remarkable at all at Nucor. According to an officer of the company, "It happens all the time." The story reflects the selfless, boundaryless behaviors and tradition of teammate ownership (centered around meeting goals for the production of high-quality steel) that have been important to Nucor's success. In return, the organization has developed and protected its teammates over the years. To avoid layoffs, it has even sent mill teammates into the field to meet with and help sell steel to (somewhat surprised) customers during the great recession of 2008 when demand for specialty steel was down and production at the mill was slow.

The term *boundaryless* is not heard around Nucor. But note the electricians' loyalty to the company, not just their particular steel mill. And notice as well the very low barrier between production and sales when falling markets demanded it. It helps explain why a small company opening its first minimill in 1969 grew to become the largest steel company in the United States.

MEASURE TO PREDICT: TODAY'S CULTURE = TOMORROW'S PERFORMANCE

The study I carried out several years ago in a global services organization, described in chapter 3, concluded that nearly 40 percent of the difference in operating income among similar businesses with significant numbers of customer-facing employees could be traced to differences in culture. You may recall that I purposely asked the company's management not to tell me how well each of the organizations I studied was doing in financial terms. Instead, they provided me with several pieces of nonfinancial operating information with which I could profile the health of the culture of each operating entity over two years. Using that data, I then predicted the relative operating income (in terms of percentage point differentials) of each entity with a high degree of accuracy.

There was no trick to this. I was merely applying what we know about how today's culture affects tomorrow's performance, using elements of the culture profit model shown in figure 3.1. In terms much simpler than those discussed in chapter 3, the relationships are:

Today's organization culture → Employee engagement → Customer engagement → Tomorrow's sales and profit[22]

Even more simply, today's culture = tomorrow's sales and profit. It may take months or even several quarters of operations for the relationship to play out, but it will play out. It requires that we measure and act on the right things.

THE CULTURE-BALANCED SCORECARD

Many organizations today still collect and manage the wrong information. Too much attention is paid to financial measures and too little is paid to measures of an organization's culture. Don't get me wrong—both are often measured. But it's the financial information that gets attention in everything from meetings with investment analysts to performance reviews and the allocation of rewards to managers.

What we're talking about here lends itself nicely to the concept of the balanced scorecard in which both financial and nonfinancial measures are reported periodically.[23] It's a useful tool if greater attention is paid to the nonfinancial measures than to the financial. Why? Data describing sales and profit performance is history. The predictors of the future are dimensions of employee and customer engagement. In some industries, these are supplemented by measures of such things as innovation and safety, depending on their importance in the long-term success of the organization.

THE POWER OF PREDICTION

Think about it. If we can measure an organization's current culture, we can predict its future performance with a substantial measure of confidence *not even knowing what the strategy is going to be.* Whatever the strategy, we can be assured that it will get executed as well as possible in an organization with an effective culture. The existence of an effective culture will enable the organization to shift from one strategy to another. That's a powerful resource for a leader. It's equally powerful for employees and investors.

Are we measuring the right things? That's a problem. In the study cited in chapter 3, I specified thirty-five pieces of non-financial information for which I would either need data or, failing its existence, management estimates. As it turned out, the availability of the data varied greatly: eleven pieces were available and easy to get; two could be found and were easy to get; ten pieces of information were available somewhere in the organization but were relatively difficult to get; and twelve pieces of data—fully one-third—did not exist and had to be estimated.

For management purposes, all that's needed are a few pieces of information tracked periodically and managed for trend improvement. For practical purposes, efforts to track the trends shown in figure 8.1 will be sufficient to predict the direction and rough magnitude of future success.

You'll recognize the nature and layout of measures shown in figure 8.1 as a simplified version of relationships described in chapters 3 and 4. Each can be assessed using a set of questions

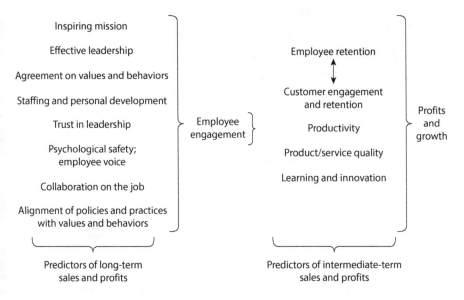

Inspiring mission

Effective leadership

Agreement on values and behaviors

Staffing and personal development

Trust in leadership

Psychological safety;
employee voice

Collaboration on the job

Alignment of policies and practices
with values and behaviors

Employee
engagement

Employee retention

Customer engagement
and retention

Productivity

Product/service quality

Learning and innovation

Profits
and
growth

Predictors of long-term
sales and profits

Predictors of intermediate-term
sales and profits

FIGURE 8.1 The culture balanced scorecard

shown in the appendix. Some can be measured in a periodic engagement survey of the type employed by many organizations today. Responses to other questions will have to be assessed somewhat subjectively by managers and employees. That act alone may encourage highly useful conversations of the type needed to sensitize leaders to what is going on in the organization.

MAKE TIME FOR CULTURE PLANNING

Strategic planning is exciting stuff. Courses are taught about it in business school. Planning and executing strategies occupy the minds and time of leaders. Books written about it are best-sellers. Too often, however, these efforts drive out time and effort devoted to culture planning and execution.

The two kinds of planning and execution require very different approaches. Strategic planning requires a block of time; the execution of a strategy requires total devotion at important moments. In contrast, culture planning is best done daily, with constant attention to execution over a day. It may require no more than five to ten minutes of a leader's time, preferably at the start of the day. It involves nothing more than reviewing the day's activities to reflect on how decisions to be made and actions to be carried out can be implemented in ways that violate or reinforce shared values and behaviors. Ideas implanted in the subconscious during the short, personal planning session will come to mind at the appropriate times and in ways that make culture-conscious leadership appear to be spontaneous. Such time for reflection is never wasted; it provides a reminder of what's important, whether or not the anticipated issues and actions arise. Periodically, the time can be used for self-evaluation, reviewing just three questions:

- What important decisions will I face today?
- What's the potential of each for reinforcing or negatively affecting the organization's culture?
- Regardless of the decision, what can I do to ensure that the culture is reinforced?

Think of this as an opportunity to huddle with yourself. It's the equivalent of the huddles that take place among employees

at the start of their work shifts in companies such as the Ritz
Carlton and Caesar's Entertainment. It reminds them of what
is coming up that day and how to deal with it.

KEEP TELLING THOSE STORIES

Stories memorialize a culture. They remind people of why and
how things were done in the past that have led to a successful present. They help explain current customs and behaviors.
They provide an introduction to newcomers that adds color to
complement dry policies and practices. We've said it before: to
preserve shared values at the core of a culture, leaders tell stories
and encourage others to tell them about organizational heroes
who put the organization above their interests. One can learn
a lot about a culture and honored behaviors by the stories told
and retold.

An example of such a story is one told by former Google
CEO Eric Schmidt:

One Friday afternoon in May 2002, (company co-founder)
Larry Page was playing around on the Google site, typing in
search terms and seeing what sort of results and ads he'd get
back. He wasn't happy with what he saw. . . . Some of the
ads were completely unrelated to the search. . . . In a normal company, the CEO, seeing a bad product, would call the
person in charge of the product. There would be a meeting or
two or three. . . . Instead, he printed out the pages containing the results he didn't like, highlighted the offending ads,

posted them on a bulletin board on the wall of the kitchen by the pool table, and wrote THESE ADS SUCK in big letters across the top. Then he went home. . . . At 5:05 a.m. the following Monday . . . Jeff Dean sent out an email. He and four colleagues . . . had seen Larry's note on the wall. . . . (Dean's email) included a detailed analysis of why the problem was occurring, described a solution, included a link to a prototype implementation of the solution the five had coded over the weekend. . . . And the kicker? Jeff and team weren't even on the ads team. . . . It was the culture that attracted . . . these five engineers . . . to the company in the first place.[24]

The actions of Dean's informal and impromptu team reflected what Google's leaders have always valued most—independent thought, initiative, teaming, and accountability.

■ ■ ■

The heroes and heroines at 3M, one of the most innovative companies in the world, are the misfits working at the funny farm, the company's product development laboratory. The typical story is about someone who is told to stop working on an idea, continues to do it secretively, and comes up with a great new product. It's about people like Spencer Silver, a chemist who came up with an adhesive that didn't stick very well, refused to put it aside completely and shared it with Art Fry, who thought of it when his hymnal bookmark fell out during choir rehearsal. He recalled the adhesive "mistake" that Spencer had shared with him five years earlier, worked on the product in

his free time, and came up with Post-it Notes. The story empha-
sizes the values of self-direction—a basic rule of management
at 3M—and collaboration that has helped 3M maintain its reputation for innovation.[25] A tolerance for "educated mistakes"
perhaps grows out of the fact that 3M, then Minnesota Mining
& Manufacturing, was founded on a mistake, the acquisition
of land that contained the wrong kind of abrasive for making
the sandpaper that was to become one of the company's most
important products.[26]

■ ■ ■

At the mutual fund giant Vanguard Group, the story may be
about Mabel Yu, an investment manager who wouldn't invest
in anything for which she couldn't adequately assess risk.[27] That
included the derivatives represented as low-risk AAA-rated
securities that were being created and marketed by Wall Street's
most reputable firms. These were the same securities that helped
trigger the great recession of 2008. She may have been ridiculed
by the financial sophisticates of Wall Street and failed to realize
some short-term profit, but she persevered, acting out the organization's bias for conservative investment practices. As a result,
Vanguard largely avoided one of the causes of poor investment performance during the recession. Yu's accomplishment
reflected the organization's values in several ways, including the
value placed on dissent and the notion that "every Vanguard
'crew member' is capable of making a contribution."[28]

The story doesn't end there. Chairman John Bogle recognized her contribution in a typically low-key Vanguard manner

by taking her to lunch one day in the company cafeteria. So the story goes, she ordered a salad—one of the least expensive items on the menu. That's important to the story because it is intended to reflect adherence to the company's core value of frugality, one that has produced the low costs that have helped the company maintain its leadership of the mutual fund industry. Yu's accomplishment was bigger news outside the Vanguard Group than inside—a reflection of the organization's reluctance to create stars among its ranks.

■ ■ ■

Although it happened on August 25, 2000, Linda Brown's experience and how she handled it still sticks in my mind. As a customer service supervisor at Southwest Airlines' check-in counter in Kansas City on an extremely hot day, she observed a counter agent confronting a potentially difficult situation. An elderly man in a wheelchair with a valid ticket on Flight 1533 to Oakland had been left at the counter by several acquaintances. He smelled so badly that he was in no condition to board the flight. With Southwest's other Customers in mind, Brown knew she couldn't let him board in that condition. On the other hand, the potential for a public relations disaster if she refused to let him board loomed large in her mind. She had seconds to act. Thinking quickly, she assured him that she would get him on his way (thus relieving anxiety) but that she would need his help putting on fresh clothes that her team members would contribute. With that assurance, he agreed to prepare for the flight. According to a report of the incident in Southwest's *LuvLines*,

"As arrangements were being made to assist the Customer with some fresh clothes so he could travel, he soiled himself. . . . Brown quickly volunteered to go to the store (at the airport) to purchase the necessary hygiene items, including Depends adult diapers. When Linda returned, she cleaned the gentleman and got him ready for his flight. Just before boarding, the gentleman experienced the same problem again, and Linda had to repeat the entire cleaning process."[29] The Customer made his flight. Brown and her team members (with team responsibility for ensuring on-time departures) knew they had the authority to do all of this. Their actions reflected the long-held belief in Southwest's culture to "do whatever you feel comfortable doing for a Customer."

■ ■ ■

Long-time members of the Harvard Business School faculty still tell about what happened during the Blizzard of 1978, one of the worst in history. By the governor's edict, all roads were closed to nonemergency travel in the Boston area. Was that enough to close HBS, particularly its executive development programs whose participants were snowed in on campus anyway? No. In anticipation of the storm, Professor Martin Marshall slept in his office all night to be available the next morning. Early the next morning, Professor John Dearden put on his cross-country skis and skied twelve miles from his home to campus before class. Dean Lawrence Fouraker, a long-time member of the faculty before becoming dean, awakened to find that the doors to the dean's house on campus were snowed shut.

There was only one thing to do— he climbed out of an upstairs window, slid down the roof into a snowbank, and headed off to class. The program proceeded on schedule, thanks to the fact that Marshall, Dearden, and Fouraker had put the organization before their interests. The story reminds potentially self-centered academics that at this institution, those who put students and the organization ahead of their interests are remembered for what they do.

Are these stories completely accurate? Probably not. Like my own and those of my long-departed grandfather, they get better with each telling. The stories may change over time to reflect the values and behaviors shared by members of the organization. And they are used by effective leaders to help communicate and reinforce the essence of cultures that fuel performance.

I've wrapped up my brief tour of how organizations compete through culture with a cafeteria of examples of leadership behaviors supportive of the effort. Unlike the actions to achieve culture change in chapter 7—a recipe for success if steps are followed in the proper order—efforts described in this chapter may be employed in various combinations to fit the situation. I've never observed a leader engaged in all these efforts at the same time. But they provide a checklist of possible behaviors that have been found useful by effective leaders. The efforts are not particularly idiosyncratic, applicable to leaders only with certain personalities and behavioral characteristics. Above all, they don't require a certain charisma. With practice, all can contribute to a successful formula for leading an organization desirous of winning from within.

IF YOU REMEMBER NOTHING ELSE . . .

- Change is the province of leadership. Without a leader's passionate support, forget about trying to reshape an organization's culture.
- Live the culture; make and execute decisions that are seen as fair in the context of a set of shared values and behaviors.
- Practice servant leadership.
- Serve as cheerleader, conscience, and coach.
- Maintain high visibility to create opportunities for listening and responding.
- Practice no-surprises leadership to build trust.
- Measure to predict tomorrow's performance.
- Reward listening and teaching.
- Make time for culture planning.
- Keep telling those stories.

Appendix

A ROBUST CULTURE-BASED BALANCED SCORECARD AUDIT

THE UNDERLYING notion for this audit is that:

Today's organization culture → Employee engagement →
Customer engagement → Tomorrow's sales and profit.

It may take months or even several quarters of operations for
the relationship to play out, but it will play out. What we're
talking about here lends itself nicely to the concept of a balanced
scorecard in which both financial and nonfinancial measures
are taken and reported periodically.[1] Figure AP.1, seen earlier
as figure 8.1, is one such scorecard.

For management purposes, what is needed are periodic estimates of performance on eight contributors to six quantitative
outcomes, beginning with employee engagement. *Obtaining
these estimates with some degree of consistency from one time period
to the next will be a challenge,* one that nevertheless can lead to a
better understanding of an organization's current nonfinancial
performance to be used to predict its future performance.

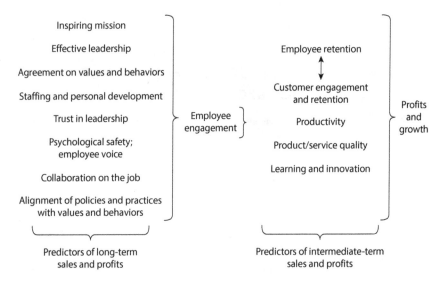

FIGURE AP.1 The culture balanced scorecard

Each of the measures shown here can be assessed using a set of questions shown below. Some can be measured in a periodic engagement survey of the type employed by many of our organizations today. Responses to other questions will have to be assessed somewhat subjectively by managers, employees, and potential investors. That act alone may encourage highly useful conversations of the type needed to sensitize leaders to what is going on in the organization.

THE CULTURE AUDIT QUESTIONNAIRE

After considering responses to the set of questions listed for each of the following fourteen dimensions, arrive at *one score for each dimension* on a 1 (weak) to 9 (strong) basis, using information obtained from surveys, conversations, and your experiences and perceptions as the leader of an organization.

1. Mission:

    How inspiring is the mission to potential and current employees?

    How visible is the mission in publications and around the company?

    To what degree does the mission provide latitude and opportunities for additional products, services, and results to be delivered to clients?

    Score: _____

2. Leadership:

    What's the relative emphasis placed on managing by the values and behaviors as opposed to the emphasis on just making the numbers?

    What importance is placed on personally acting out the shared values and behaviors on which the culture depends?

    To what extent does the leadership team believe that culture is a vital element in the current and potential success of the organization?

    Score: _____

3. Agreement on values and behaviors:

    To what extent are employees aware of the organization's shared values and behaviors?

    To what extent do they employ them in their daily work?

Are values and behaviors taken into consideration in
making major decisions?

Score: _____

4. Staffing and personal development:

How much effort is devoted to finding and preparing
people who identify with the organization's mission
and culture?

How heavy is the emphasis on hiring for attitude,
training for skills?

To what extent are jobs (especially those requiring
creativity) staffed with people of varying backgrounds,
knowledge, and points of view?

How much emphasis is placed on personal development
both in the workplace and through other means?

Score: _____

5. Trust in leadership:

To what extent do leaders practice no-surprises leadership?

To what extent are leaders' decisions regarding people
viewed as fair?

What are the trends in survey measures of the degree to
which employees trust their peers, their immediate
boss, and the organization (or its leaders) as a whole?

Score: _____

6. Psychological safety and employee voice:

To what degree (a) are people encouraged to speak out?
and (b) do they do it?

How good are managers at listening and responding?

To what degree are various forms of transparency
employed usefully to keep people informed about their
progress and that of the organization?

Score: _____

7. Collaboration on the job:

How heavy is the reliance on people working in teams?

To what extent are best-practice efforts organized and
supported?

What evidence is there of boundaryless behavior?

Score: _____

8. Alignment of policies and practices with culture:

Are managers evaluated and rewarded, among other
things, on their ability to manage by the agreed-upon
shared values and accepted behaviors?

To what degree do incentives encourage behaviors
consistent with the culture (e.g., team-based incentives
to encourage collaboration)?

Is there some mechanism (process) in place for reviewing
the consistency of decisions with the organization's
shared values and accepted behaviors?

Score: _____

9. Employee engagement:

Does the organization measure employee engagement
levels regularly and consistently?

If so, what are significant trends in employee engagement?

If not, is there other evidence of a high degree of
employee engagement (identification with the mission,
shared values, and behaviors; intent to remain with
the organization, offering suggestions for new ways of
doing things, etc.)?

Score: _____

10. Employee retention:

Is employee retention at various levels measured
systematically? If so, what are important trends
in it?

Are employees relied on heavily for referrals of new
employees? Is this encouraged and tracked?

How well are employee exits handled?

Score: _____

11. Customer retention and engagement:

Is customer retention measured systematically? If so, what
are important trends in it?

Are customers relied on heavily for referrals of new
business? Is this encouraged and tracked?

To what degree do customers offer suggestions for new
processes or products?

Score: _____

12. Productivity:

How does productivity compare with that of major
competitors?

What are the trends in productivity?

Score: _____

13. Product/service quality:

Is product/service quality measured? If so, what are the trends in quality?

To what degree does the organization concentrate on continuous quality improvement?

For service organizations, what is the quality and speed of service recovery?

Score: _____

14. Learning and innovation:

What is the percentage of sales realized from products/services developed in the past five years?

What is the trend in this measure?

How much emphasis is placed on learning and creative activity with time allocated for those activities?

Score: _____

Total Score (Culture Index):

_____

INTERPRETATION OF RESULTS

The culture index reflects a profit model based on several research studies. Its components can be mapped as follows:

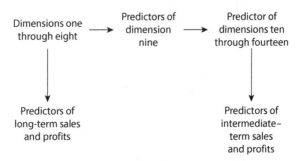

The first eight dimensions, to the extent that they influence the others, are critical to the evaluation. Trends in assessments of each of these dimensions can be used in evaluating progress toward performance goals.

If the emphasis is on near-term or intermediate-term sales and profits, extra weight can be given to two dimensions: employee retention and client retention and engagement.

If the emphasis is on long-term performance, extra weighting can be given to product/service quality and learning and innovation. The result can be considered along with results from the first eight dimensions.

SCORING AND ANALYSIS OF RESULTS

In calculating results, the objective is to obtain an average of the scores. Thus, the result will be a final score in the range of 1 to 9.

The dimensions of the index are not equally important. Their importance differs in various industries or types of organizations. There is little research to suggest the appropriate weight of these elements. Managerial judgment will be required. Based on personal work (and biases), the following weights might be considered:

Double weight for leadership and engagement in all appraisals.

Double weight for staffing and product/service quality in service organizations with a high proportion of employees in face-to-face contact with customers.

Double weight for learning and innovation in organizations such as those in rapidly changing (e.g., high-tech) industries.

Dimensions that are double-weighted will be entered twice into the calculation. As a result, in calculating an overall value for all categories, an organization with two double-weighted dimensions will have sixteen numbers entered into the numerator. Its results will be divided by sixteen, not fourteen, in order to make all results comparable.

It may be of greatest value to calculate an average for the first eight dimensions (the inputs), then relate that to changes in dimensions nine through fourteen (the results).

The audit will yield an absolute score between 1 and 9. Based on limited testing in other organizations, consider a composite score between 5 and 6 to be fair, one between 6 and 7 to be good, and one from 7 to 8 to be very good. Over 8 is off the charts. The best use of such scores, however, is to track trends based on periodic (typically annual) use of the audit.

More work remains to be done to calibrate the impact of these fourteen dimensions on financial outcomes. However,

studies have shown that the best places to work achieve performance levels that produce a five-percentage-point advantage in
ROI over other firms. If the best places to work are judged to
score 8.0 or more on the 9-point scale, while other firms score
around 6.0, then a reasonable working estimate is that a one-
tenth of a point change in total average score from one period to
the next *on the first eight dimensions* will raise or lower profit on
investment by approximately a quarter of a percentage point, or
25 basis points, *in the long-term*, with a lag of twelve to eighteen
months, depending on the nature of the business. With a lag
time of six to nine months, it should produce a similar direc-
tional change in scores for dimension nine, employee engagement. If the effects of the change have already reached the ninth
dimension, a change of one-tenth of one point in this dimension may well be reflected in a similar change of one-quarter
of a percentage point or twenty-five basis points in return on
investment *in the short-term*, with a lag in most cases of no more
than six to nine months for most businesses.

CAVEATS

The precision of any management and investment tool of this
kind can be questioned legitimately. Trends provided by periodic assessments are much more useful and valid than measurements at any one point in time.

This kind of device will always be improved through use.
To date, the culture audit shown here has received limited use.
With use, results and their interpretations will improve.

Where estimates are provided by evaluators (as opposed to survey results or other quantitative sources based on large samples of respondents) there is always the challenge of consistency in carrying out evaluations from one time period to the next. It will depend on the standards of the evaluator(s). The questions for each dimension of the model are intended to prepare an evaluator to make as accurate an assessment as possible and minimize differences in personal standards, but those differences will remain. If possible, the average of assessments by two or three evaluators will help to reduce this kind of bias and at the same time encourage a discussion of standards among evaluators.

Questions will arise about how to establish a base value for a dimension. That is, how do we translate a 5.5 out of a perfect 7.0 on an employee retention survey to the 9-point scales used here? Typically, purveyors of such surveys will provide some basis for calibration (that is, just how good a score of 5.5 is among scores for various organizations), but experience in using the measures as well as judgment will be required to establish a base for equating survey results.

This is an ambitious effort to predict an organization's future performance based on elements of its culture. It is a work in progress. It will always require judgment and experience in use. But much of it is based on research results. Think of it both as a practical tool and as the basis for additional learning.

NOTES

INTRODUCTION

1. See especially Jeffrey Pfeffer, *Leadership BS: Fixing Workplaces and Careers One Truth at a Time* (New York: HarperBusiness, 2015).

2. Jim Collins, *Good to Great: Why Some Companies Make the Leap . . . and Others Don't* (New York: HarperCollins, 2001).

3. Among other sources, see especially Geert Hofstede, *Culture's Consequences: International Differences in Work-Related Values*, abridged ed. (Newbury Park, CA: Sage, 1980); and Richard D. Lewis, *When Cultures Collide: Leading Across Cultures* (Boston: Nicholas Brealey International, 2006).

4. James Heskett, *The Culture Cycle: How to Shape the Unseen Force That Transforms Performance* (Upper Saddle River, NJ: FT Press, 2012), especially 219–249.

5. Marc Benioff, "Marc Benioff Talks Salesforce-AT&T Deal, Office Health Safety and Online Media Regulation," #CNBC, May 29, 2020, YouTube video, 9:38, https://www.youtube.com/watch?v=Oub322f8gOg, quote at 5:18.

6. See, for example, Jeremy Rifkin, *The Third Industrial Revolution: How Lateral Power Is Transforming Energy, the Economy, and the World* (New York: St. Martin's, 2011).

1. CULTURE: THE NEARLY PERFECT COMPETITIVE WEAPON

1. Catherine Yoshimoto and Ed Frauenheim, "The Best Companies to Work For Are Beating the Market," Fortune.com, February 27, 2018, https://fortune.com/the-best-companies-to-work-for-are-beating-the-market.
2. Eric Schmidt and Jonathan Rosenberg with Alan Eagle, *How Google Works* (New York: Grand Central, 2014), 23, 29.
3. Tony Hsieh, *Delivering Happiness: A Path to Profits, Passion, and Purpose* (New York: Business Plus, 2010), 154.
4. Ray Dalio, *Principles* (New York: Simon & Schuster, 2017), 299.
5. Louis V. Gerstner Jr., *Who Says Elephants Can't Dance? Inside IBM's Historic Turnaround* (New York: HarperCollins, 2002), 181, 182.
6. https://www.nucorsteel.com, accessed May 2010. The page is no longer available.
7. The first of several Harvard Business School cases about Southwest Airlines was written by Christopher Lovelock and appeared in 1975. They were followed by several that I authored or coauthored.
8. Herb Kelleher, chairman emeritus, Southwest Airlines, interview by author, Dallas, TX, December 2008.
9. This is an arbitrary short list drawn from a much longer list of companies with equally remarkable cultures. They are found at the intersection of survey findings by organizations such as Glassdoor and the Great Places to Work Institute, on the one hand, and J. D. Power and Bloomburg Businessweek customer service surveys, on the other. Service organizations included on the list are those identified in a study cited in James L. Heskett, W. Earl Sasser Jr., and Leonard A. Schlesinger, *What Great Service Leaders Know and Do* (Oakland, CA: Berrett-Koehler, 2015), 54. I have purposely limited the list to companies that have been in operation for twenty years or more. There are a number of younger companies that promise to develop equally interesting and effective cultures.
10. John R. Graham, Campbell R. Harey, Jillian Popadak, and Shivaram Rajgopal, "Corporate Culture: Evidence from the Field," working paper, 27th Annual Conference on Financial Economics and Accounting Paper, Colombia Business School Research Paper No. 16-49, New York, June 26, 2019, http://ssrn.com/abstract=2805602.
11. A 2016 estimate of the Association of Certified Fraud Examiners, referenced in Evans Ocansey and Josephine Ganu, "The Role of Corporate

Culture in Managing Occupational Fraud," *Research Journal of Finance and Accounting* 8, no. 24 (December 2017).

12. See John Doerr, *Measure What Matters: How Google, Bono, and the Gates Foundation Rock the World with OKRs* (New York: Portfolio, 2018), 213. Grove writes, "The point is that a strong and positive corporate culture is absolutely essential." See Andrew S. Grove, *High Output Management* (New York: Penguin, 1983), 135.

13. John P. Kotter and James L. Heskett, *Corporate Culture and Performance* (New York: Free Press, 1992).

14. Edgar H. Schein, *Organization Culture and Leadership* (San Francisco: Jossey-Bass, 1985), 33.

15. Some attribute a version of this saying, "culture eats strategy for breakfast," to the late Peter Drucker, but neither Quote Investigator nor I can find evidence of this. The earliest reference to the remark appears in 2000. By 2011, it was being attributed to Drucker, who died in 2005. Quote Investigator, s.v. "Culture Eats Strategy for Breakfast," May 23, 2017, https.//quoteinvestigator.com/2017/05/23/culture-eats-strategy-for-breakfast.

16. The case for simultaneously changing both the "economic model" and the "organizational model" (including culture) strategy is well made in Michael Beer, *High Commitment, High Performance: How to Build a Resilient Organization for Sustained Advantage* (San Francisco: Jossey-Bass, 2009), 295–325.

17. Rita Gunther McGrath, *The End of Competitive Advantage: How to Keep Your Strategy Moving as Fast as Your Business* (Boston: Harvard Business Review Press, 2013).

18. Ben Horowitz, *What You Do Is Who You Are: How to Create Your Business Culture* (New York: Harper Collins, 2019), 3.

19. Graham, Harey, Popadak, and Rajgopal, "Corporate Culture."

20. https://comparably.com, accessed November 15, 2020.

2. CULTURE ENGAGES EMPLOYEES

1. Tony Hsieh, *Delivering Happiness: A Path to Profits, Passion, and Purpose* (New York: Hachette, 2010), 39.

2. Hsieh, *Delivering Happiness*, 47–48.

3. Hsieh, *Delivering Happiness*, 48.

4. Noam Wasserman, *The Founder's Dilemmas: Anticipating and Avoiding the Pitfalls That Can Sink a Startup* (Princeton, NJ: Princeton University Press, 2012).

5. Marc Benioff and Carlye Adler, *Behind the Cloud: The Untold Story of How Salesforce.com Went from Idea to Billion-Dollar Company—and Revolutionized an Industry* (San Francisco: Jossey-Bass, 2009), 11.

6. Marc Benioff and Monica Langley, *Trailblazer: The Power of Business as the Greatest Platform for Change* (New York: Random House, 2019), 22.

7. Quoted in Robert Stringer, *Culture.com: How the Best Startups Make It Happen* (Boston: Crimson Seed Capital Publishing, 2017), 10.

8. Marc Benioff and Monica Langley, *Trailblazer*, 131.

9. See James C. Collins and Jerry I. Porras, *Built to Last: Successful Habits of Visionary Companies* (New York: Harper Business, 1994).

10. "Create a Proven Employee Engagement Strategy," Gallup, Inc., 2021, https://advise.gallup.com/employee/engagement.

11. Jason Flynn and Arthur H. Mazor, "The Employee Experience: Culture, Engagement, and Beyond," 2017 Global Human Capital Trends, Deloitte, 2017, www2.deloitte.com.

12. Gallup, Inc., *State of the Global Workplace* (New York: Gallup Press, 2017).

13. Randall Beck and Jim Harter, "Managers Account for 70 Percent of Variance in Employee Engagement," *Gallup Business Journal* (April 2015).

14. These components of culture were first set forth by Edgar Schein in his book, *Organizational Culture and Leadership* (San Francisco: Jossey-Bass, 1991).

15. Roar V. Bonim, "How Airbnb Became the World's Best Place to Work," livingroomanalytics.com, May 19, 2019, accessed May 22, 2021. The claim is based on rankings by Glassdoor's (glassdoor.com) 2016 rankings.

16. http://www.comparably.com, accessed November 7, 2019. This vision perhaps intentionally contrasts with a famous paraphrase attributed to Nobel economist Milton Friedman that, "The business of business is business." What Friedman actually wrote is summed up in the title of his article, "The Social Responsibility of Business Is to Increase Its Profits," *New York Times Magazine*, September 13, 1970.

17. One can get a sense of what the board heard in the pages of a book by Arkadi Kuhlmann and Bruce Philp, *The Orange Code: How ING Direct Succeeded by Being a Rebel With a Cause* (Hoboken, NJ: John Wiley, 2009). Material not in quotes is a paraphrase of material on 207–221 of the book.

18. This is based on an estimated cost of recruiting and hiring by the Society of Human Resource Management in 2016 of $4,129 per person hired ("Average Cost-per-Hire for Companies Is $4,129," shrm.org, accessed December 13, 2019) multiplied by the 69 million employees hired in the United States in the twelve months ending September 30, 2019 (bls.gov).

19. Corporate Leadership Council, *Driving Employee Performance and Retention Through Engagement: A Quantitative Analysis of the Effectiveness of Employee Engagement Strategies* (Washington, London, and New Delhi: Corporate Executive Board, 2004).
20. Corporate Leadership Council, *Driving Employee Performance.*
21. Claes Fornell, Sunil Mithas, Forrest V. Morgenson III, and M. S. Krishnan, "Customer Satisfaction and Stock Prices: High Returns, Low Risk," *Journal of Marketing* (January 2006): 3–14.
22. Catherine Yoshimoto and Ed Frauenheim, "The Best Companies to Work For Are Beating the Market," February 27, 2018, https://fortune.com /the-best-companies-to-work-for-are-beating-the-market.

3. HOW CULTURE DRIVES PERFORMANCE: FOLLOW THE MONEY

1. John R. Graham, Campbell R. Harey, Jillian Popadak, and Shivaram Rajgopal, "Corporate Culture: Evidence from the Field" working paper, 27th Annual Conference on Financial Economics and Accounting Paper, Colombia Business School Research Paper No. 16-49, New York, NY, June 26, 2019, http://ssrn.com/abstract=2805602.
2. As the numbers will show, this was not the case in the two branches shown in my example. However, in most of the other pairs of branches included in my study, it did prove to be the case.
3. Heather Boushey and Sarah Jane Glynn, "There Are Significant Business Costs to Replacing Employees," Center for American Progress, December 16, 2012, americanprogress.org.
4. Typical of these studies is one that concluded that employees with high engagement scores were 2.5 times more likely to remain on the job for the next six months than their less engaged counterparts. Source: Shad Foos, vice president of marketing, service management group, in an email message to the author, February 10, 2015.
5. Shad Foos, email to the author.
6. Nate Dvorak and Ryan Pendell, "Culture Wins By Getting the Most Out of People," Gallup, July 31, 2018, https://www.gallup.com/workplace /238052/culture-wins-getting-people.aspx.
7. James L. Heskett, W. Earl Sasser, and Leonard A. Schlesinger, *The Service Profit Chain: How Leading Companies Link Profit and Growth to Loyalty, Satisfaction, and Value* (New York: Free Press, 1997).

8. Daniel Zhao, "Happy Employees, Satisfied Customers: The Link Between Glassdoor Reviews and Customer Satisfaction," Glassdoor, August 7, 2019, https://www.glassdoor.com/research/employee-reviews-customer -satisfaction/#.

9. Highly engaged employees and customers can be thought of as "owners," in a psychological sense. See James L. Heskett, W. Earl Sasser, and Joe Wheeler, *The Ownership Quotient: Putting the Service Profit Chain to Work for Unbeatable Competitive Advantage* (Boston: Harvard Business Press, 2008).

10. Frederick F. Reichheld and W. Earl Sasser Jr., "Zero Defections: Quality Comes to Services," *Harvard Business Review*, September–October 1990, 105–111. Reichheld subsequently expanded on these ideas in his book, *The Loyalty Effect: The Hidden Force Behind Growth, Profits, and Lasting Value* (Boston: Harvard Business School Press, 1996), especially 33–62, leading to the development of the Net Promoter Score now employed by thousands of organizations worldwide.

11. It didn't stop there. Seven star (and diamond, the next highest level of value) customers actually had made 20 percent more recommendations to friends to visit Harrah's properties than gold customers, resulting in 32 percent more new customer recruits with an estimated lifetime value to the company 73 percent greater than those recruited by gold customers. Source: James L. Heskett, W. Earl Sasser, and Joe Wheeler, *The Ownership Quotient.*

12. Most of this evidence is anecdotal, drawn from examples of innovative organizations. For example, see profiles of leading centers of innovation such as 3M in my book, *The Culture Cycle: How to Shape the Unseen Force That Transforms Performance* (Englewood Cliffs, NJ: Pearson, 2012), 182–190; the Mayo Clinic in Leonard L. Berry and Kent D. Seltman, *Management Lessons from Mayo Clinic: Inside One of the World's Most Admired Service Organizations* (New York: McGraw-Hill, 2008); and Google, W. L. Gore, and Whole Foods Market in Gary Hamel, *The Future of Management* (Boston: Harvard Business School Press, 2007).

13. Evans O. N. D. Ocansey and Josephine Ganu, "The Role of Corporate Culture in Managing Occupational Fraud," *Research Journal of Finance and Accounting* 8, no. 24 (December 2017).

14. James K. Harter, Frank L. Schmidt, and Theodore L. Hayes, "Business-Unit-Level Relationship Between Employee Satisfaction, Employee

Engagement, and Business Outcomes: A Meta-Analysis," *Journal of Applied Psychology* no. 2 (2002): 268–279.

15. Larry Bossidy and Ram Charan, *Execution: The Discipline of Getting Things Done* (New York: Crown Business, 2002), 195.

4. WHY SOME ORGANIZATIONS ENGAGE EMPLOYEES (AND CUSTOMERS) BETTER THAN OTHERS

1. Abigail Stevenson, "T-Mobile CEO Sheds Light on Major Changes Ahead to Fix a 'Broken, Arrogant Industry," February 14, 2017, https://www.cnbc.com/2017/02/14/t-mobile-ceo-tells-cramer-he-wants-to-fix-a-broken-arrogant-industry.html.

2. T-Mobile.com, accessed September 15, 2019.

3. Richard Feloni, "T-Mobile's CEO Says Reinventing Himself Was Key to Transforming the Company's Culture," *Business Insider*, October 17, 2016, https://www.businessinsider.com/t-mobile-ceo-john-legere-company-culture-2016-10.

4. Mike McNamee, "Credit Card Revolutionary," *Stanford Business*, May 2001, 23.

5. Note the custom of capitalizing both *Employee* and *Customer* at Southwest. It's a good example of an artifact of culture at work. See figure 2.1.

6. The actual number hired in one day turned out to be much smaller than this. However, the hiring goal was met in a relatively short time, raising the potential for the kind of stress on a company's culture that is always associated with rapid growth.

7. See, for example, findings from one of the largest studies of its type by Leonard A. Schlesinger and Jeffrey Zornitsky, "Job Satisfaction, Service Capability, and Customer Satisfaction: An Examination of Linkages and Management Implications," *Human Resource Planning* 14, no. 2: 141–149.

8. See Francis Fukuyama, *Trust: The Social Virtues and The Creation of Prosperity* (New York: Simon & Schuster, 1995), especially 256–276.

9. Andrew Ross Sorkin, "Seeking a Path to Trust," *New York Times*, November 12, 2019, F1. See also, Stephen M. R. Covey with Rebecca R. Merrill, *The Speed of Trust: The One Thing That Changes Everything* (New York: Simon & Schuster, 2006).

10. See Kurt Dirks and Donald L. Ferrin, "Trust in Leadership: Meta-Analytic Findings and Implications for Research and Practice," *Journal of Applied Psychology* 87, no. 4 (September 2002): 611–628.

11. Amy C. Edmondson, *The Fearless Organization: Creating Psychological Safety in the Workplace for Learning, Innovation, and Growth* (Hoboken, NJ: John Wiley, 2017).

12. Edmondson, *The Fearless Organization*.

13. Corporate Leadership Council, *Driving Employee Performance and Retention Through Engagement: A Quantitative Analysis of the Effectiveness of Employee Engagement Strategies* (Corporate Executive Board, 2004), 17.

14. Jody Hoffer Gittell and Rogelio Oliva, "Southwest Airlines in Baltimore," HBS Case No. 9-602-956 (Boston: Harvard Business School, 2002), 3.

15. This description is based on personal experience as an instructor at a Châteauform' facility.

16. When employees are asked both whether they trust their top management in headquarters and their immediate boss, levels of trust for one's immediate boss are significantly higher.

17. Ben Wigert and Ellyn Maese, "How Your Manager Experience Shapes Your Employee Experience," Gallup Workplace, July 9, 2019, https://www.gallup.com/workplace/259469/manager-experience-shapes-employee-experience.aspx.

18. See Daniel Coyle, *The Culture Code: The Secrets of Highly Successful Groups* (New York: Penguin, 2018), especially 74–88, for many practical suggestions about what it takes to build employee belonging essential for engagement.

19. Daniel Cable, Francisca Gino, and Bradley Staats, "Breaking Them In or Revealing Their Best? Reframing Socialization Around Newcomer Self-Expression," *Administrative Science Quarterly* 58, no. 1 (2013): 1–36.

20. Jeffrey Pfeffer, "Building Sustainable Organizations: The Human Factor," *Academy of Management Perspectives* 24, no. 1 (November 30, 2017): https://journals.aom.org/doi/abs/10.5465/amp.24.1.34.

21. See, for example, Natalie Peart, "Making Work Less Stressful and More Engaging for Your Employees," *Harvard Business Review*, November 5, 2019.

22. bls.gov., accessed December 11, 2019.

23. Lizzie Widdicombe, "Rate Your Boss!," *New Yorker*, January 22, 2018, 23.

24. Widdicombe, "Rate Your Boss!," 23.

5. HOW EFFECTIVE CULTURES ARE SUSTAINED

1. Nautical terms are the norm at Vanguard, named by founder (and sailor) John Bogle after Lord Nelson's sailing man-of-war.

2. Thomas H. Davenport and Brook Manville, *Judgment Calls: 12 Stories of Big Decisions and the Teams That Got Them Right* (Boston: Harvard Business Review Press, 2012), 157.

3. Tony Hsieh, *Delivering Happiness: A Path to Profits, Passion, and Purpose* (New York: Business Plus, 2010), especially 147–154.

4. Jean M. Phillips, "Effects of Realistic Job Previews on Multiple Organizational Outcomes: A Meta-Analysis," *Academy of Management Journal* 41 (1998): 673–690.

5. Richard L. Brandt, "Birth of a Salesman," *Wall Street Journal*, October 15, 2011.

6. See Boris Groysberg, *Chasing Stars: The Myth of Talent and the Portability of Performance* (Princeton, NJ: Princeton University Press, 2010), especially 82–84.

7. Gunter K. Stahl, Martha I. Maznevski, Andreas Voigt, and Karsten Jonsen, "Unraveling the Effect of Cultural Diversity in Teams: A Meta-Analysis of Research on Multicultural Work Groups," *Journal of International Business Studies* 41, no. 4 (2010): 690–709.

8. Roger C. Mayer, Richard S. Warr, and Jinq Zhao, "Do Pro-Diversity Policies Improve Corporate Innovation?," *Financial Management*, December 18, 2017.

9. Juliet Bourke, *Which Two Heads Are Better Than One? How Diverse Teams Create Breakthrough Ideas and Make Smarter Decisions* (Queensland: Australian Institute of Company Directors, 2016).

10. Sundaitu Dixon-Fyle, Kevin Doyle, Vivian Hunt, and Sara Prince, "Diversity Wins: How Inclusion Matters," McKinsey & Company, May 19, 2020, mckinsey.com, accessed July 26, 2020.

11. It helps explain why a Coca-Cola organization with good intentions had to announce recently that the proportion of blacks in its workforce had not increased despite a concerted effort over several years to improve it. See Jennifer Maloney and Lauren Weber, "Coke's Elusive Goal: Boosting Its Black Employees," *Wall Street Journal*, December 16, 2020.

12. Peter Eavis, "Why Not Treat Diversity Like a Profit?," *New York Times*, July 15, 2020, B1 and B3.

13. For a study of several successful organizations that are known for these traits, see Gary Hamel with Bill Breen, *The Future of Management* (Boston: Harvard Business School Press, 2007).

14. Pisano's quote is from Rhett Power, "How to Foster Innovative Thinking At Your Company," *CEOWorld Magazine*, July 24, 2019.

15. Stefan H. Thomke, *Experimentation Works: The Surprising Power of Business Experiments* (Boston: Harvard Business Review Press, 2020), 2.

16. For an extended case study of Booking.com, see Thomke, *Experimentation Works*, 153–185. For other case studies of the use of experimentation in the tech sector, see Michael Luca and Max H. Bazerman, *The Power of Experiments: Decision-Making in a Data-Driven World* (Cambridge, MA: MIT Press, 2020), especially 61–132.

17. Roger Hallowell, "Handelsbanken," (London: The Case Centre, 2020), 4, https://www.thecasecentre.org. Anders Bouvin retired in March, 2019. He was succeeded by Carina Akerstrom.

18. Lou Gerstner, "The Culture Ate Our Corporate Reputation," *Wall Street Journal*, October 3, 2016, A17.

19. Natalie Kitroeff, David Gelles, and Jack Nicas, "Boeing Rejected Safety System for 737 Max Jet, Engineer Says," *New York Times*, October 3, 2019, B1 and B4.

20. Jeffrey Swartz, "A Sharing of Strength," in Marc Benioff and Carlye Adler, *The Business of Changing the World: Twenty Great Leaders on Strategic Corporate Philanthropy* (New York: McGraw-Hill, 2007), at 45.

21. Jennifer Johnston, "Turn Your Culture Into a Competitive Advantage," Salesforce Blog, August 29, 2017, https://www.salesforce.com/content/blogs/us/en/2017/08/turn-your-culture-into-competitive-advantage.html.

22. Email communication with Sam Leyendecker, head of the culture committee at Southwest Airlines, November 13, 2019.

23. See Robert S. Kaplan and David Norton, *The Balanced Scorecard* (Boston: Harvard Business School Press, 1996).

6. CULTURE, ENGAGEMENT, AND WORK FROM ANYWHERE

1. See, for example, David Streitfeld, "White-Collar Companies Won't Rush to the Office," *New York Times*, May 11, 2020, B1. Streitfeld points out that 8 percent of workers were telecommuting at least part of the time prior to the pandemic.

2. Kate Conger, "At Facebook, Home Work Will Become Permanent," *New York Times*, May 22, 2020, B1.

3. Ben Luthi, "Almost Half of Remote Workers Report Feeling Isolated, but 81 Percent Want to Stay Remote [Survey]," FinanceBuzz, last updated October 4, 2020, https://financebuzz.com/drawbacks-remote-work-survey. This survey also identified other workers' concerns, including 49 percent who found it harder to "build relationships with co-workers," 38 percent who found it difficult to "separate work from personal life," 31 percent who felt that they experienced "different perks/benefits between in-office and remote," 30 percent who experienced "increased distractions," and 25 percent who found it. "challenging to be in a different time zone from co-workers."

4. Heidi Lynne Kurter, "How to Build an Inclusive Virtual Culture with These 4 Effective Strategies," *Forbes*, May 21, 2020, https://www.forbes.com/sites/heidilynnekurter/2020/05/21/how-to-build-an-inclusive-virtual-culture-with-these-4-effective-strategies/?sh=511a39c71062. In addition to over-communicating, Kurter suggests that managers of remote talent "champion a culture of collaboration, inspire a new language of kudos, and encourage employees to bring their whole selves (by getting to know them on a personal level)."

5. Among a number of studies documenting the increase in remote work, see Adam Osimek, "The Future of Remote Work," Upwork Global, Inc., December 20, 2020. This study documents an 87 percent increase in remote work from pre-pandemic levels and predicts that by 2025, 22 percent of the American workforce will be working remotely.

6. Dan Maher and Dan O'Brien, "The Future Came Early and It's Liquid: Critical Mass," Omnicom University Case No. OU-228, Omnicom Group, Inc., May, 2020, 1. This is the source of other material and quotes for the Critical Mass example that follow.

7. Observations about Automattic are gained from notes taken by Steve Claveski during an interview with Automattic founder, Matt Mullenweg, and presented in "The Five Levels of Remote Work—And Why You're Probably at Level 2," *Medium*, March 29, 2020, https://medium.com/swlh/the-five-levels-of-remote-work-and-why-youre-probably-at-level-2-ccaf05a25b9c.

8. Prithwiraj Choudhury and Emma Salomon, "GitLab and the Future of All-Remote Work (A)," Case No. 9-620-066, Harvard Business School Publishing, April 2, 2020, 1.

9. Email to the author from William Horner, May 7, 2020.

10. The quote is attributed to several management pundits.

7. CHANGE THE CULTURE

1. Meeting between the author and Peter Coors in Golden, Colorado, on January 10, 1991. This story appears in a somewhat different form in James L. Heskett, *The Culture Cycle: How to Shape the Unseen Force That Transforms Performance* (Englewood Cliffs, NJ: Pearson, 2012), 58. Coors has told me that if I tell this story, he will deny he said it. The Coors' executive's name in this story is disguised. The study referred to is reported in John Kotter and James L. Heskett, *Corporate Culture and Performance* (New York: The Free Press, 1992).

2. Frances Frei and Anne Morriss, *Unleashed: The Unapologetic Leader's Guide to Empowering Everyone Around You* (Boston: Harvard Business Review Press, 2020), 173.

3. Mike Isaac, "Uber's Culture of Gutsiness Under Review," *New York Times*, February 23, 2017, A1. See also Isaac's subsequent book, *Super Pumped: The Battle for Uber* (New York: Norton, 2019).

4. Adam Bryant, "We're Family, So We Can Disagree: Xerox's New Chief Tries to Redefine Its Culture," *New York Times*, February 21, 2010, B9.

5. Satya Nadella with Greg Shaw and Jill Tracie Nichols, *Hit Refresh: The Quest to Rediscover Microsoft's Soul and Imagine a Better Future for Everyone* (New York: HarperCollins, 2017).

6. John Kotter, *A Force for Change: How Leadership Differs from Management* (New York: The Free Press, 1990), especially 3–18.

7. See Michael Beer, *High Commitment, High Performance: How to Build a Resilient Organization for Sustained Advantage* (San Francisco: Jossey-Bass, 2009), 295–325.

8. Eric Schmidt and Jonathan Rosenberg with Alan Eagle, *How Google Works* (New York: Grand Central, 2014), 61.

9. Michael Beer, *Organizational Change and Development: A Systems View* (Santa Monica, CA: Goodyear Publishing, 1980).

10. Nadella, *Hit Refresh*, 66–67.

11. Tom Wolfe, *The Electric Kool-Aid Acid Test* (New York: Farrar, Straus and Giroux, 1968), 83.

12. Jim Collins, *Good to Great: Why Some Companies Make the Leap . . . and Others Don't* (New York: HarperBusiness, 2001), 41. The words in brackets reflect another Collins point but are not part of the quotation.

13. Nadella, *Hit Refresh*, 81.

14. John Doerr, *Measure What Matters: How Google, Bono, and the Gates Foundation Rock the World with OKRs* (New York: Portfolio, 2018), 227.

15. Frei and Morriss, *Unleashed*, 56.
16. Tom Ealy, "Petri Dish," LinkedIn, November 20, 2016.
17. Nadella, *Hit Refresh*, 76.
18. Nadella, *Hit Refresh*, 87.
19. Nadella, *Hit Refresh*, 88–90.
20. Adam Bryant, "Figure Out the Things You Don't Know," *New York Times*, June 5, 2016, BU2.
21. James C. Collins and Jerry I. Porras, *Built to Last: Successful Habits of Visionary Companies* (New York: Harper Business, 1994), 8.
22. Rosabeth Moss Kanter, "IBM's Values and Corporate Citizenship," Case No. 9-308-106 (Boston: Harvard Business School Publishing, September 16, 2009), 1.
23. Amy C. Edmondson, *The Fearless Organization: Creating Psychological Safety in the Workplace for Learning, Innovation, and Growth* (Hoboken, NJ: John Wiley, 2017).
24. Austin Carr and Dina Bass, "The Nadellaissance," Bloomberg Businessweek, May 6, 2019, 36–41, at 38.
25. Carr and Bass, "The Nadellaisance," 36
26. Carr and Bass, "The Nadellaissance," 41.

8. LEAD FOR COMPETITIVE ADVANTAGE THROUGH CULTURE

1. Robert Slater, *Saving Big Blue: Leadership Lessons & Turnaround Tactics of IBM's Lou Gerstner* (New York: McGraw-Hill, 1999), 93.
2. Satya Nadella with Greg Shaw and Jill Tracie Nichols, *Hit Refresh: The Quest to Rediscover Microsoft's Soul and Imagine a Better Future for Everyone* (New York: HarperCollins, 2017), 100.
3. Richard Feloni, "T-Mobile's CEO Says Reinventing Himself Was Key to Transforming the Company's Culture," Business Insider, October 17, 2016, https://www.businessinsider.in/T-Mobiles-CEO-says-reinventing-himself-was-key-to-transforming-the-companys-culture/articleshow/54906581.cms.
4. See Jim Collins, *Good to Great: Why Some Companies Make the Leap . . . and Others Don't* (New York: HarperBusiness, 2001), especially 17–40.
5. Jessica Cohen, Matt Schrimper, and Emily Taylor, "Elephant in the Room: Making a Culture Transformation Stick with Symbolic Actions," McKinsey & Co. (Leadership & Organization blog), July 29, 2019, https://www.mckinsey.com/business-functions/organization/our

-insights/the-organization-blog/elephant-in-the-room-making-a-culture
-transformation-stick-with-symbolic-actions.

6.   Eric Schmidt and Jonathan Rosenberg with Alan Eagle, *How Google Works* (New York: Grand Central, 2014), 64.

7.   Austin Carr and Dina Bass, "The Nadellaissance," Bloomberg Businessweek, May 6, 2019, 36–41, at 39.

8.   Leonard A. Schlesinger and Jeffrey Zornitsky, "Job Satisfaction, Service Capability, and Customer Satisfaction: An Examination of Linkages and Management Implications," *Human Resource Planning* 14, no. 2: 141–149.

9.   See Robert K. Greenleaf, *The Servant as Leader* (Westfield, Indiana: Greenleaf Center for Servant Leadership, 2008, revised printing).

10. Eric Schmidt, Jonathan Rosenberg, and Alan Eagle, *Trillion Dollar Coach: The Leadership Playbook of Silicon Valley's Bill Campbell* (New York: HarperCollins, 2019), xiii–xiv.

11. Cohen, Schrimper, and Taylor, "Elephant in the Room."

12. Based on author interview with former Towne Park CEO, Charles Heskett (the author's son), June 15, 2019.

13. T-Mobile. com, accessed September 10, 2019.

14. Glassdoor.com, accessed September 15, 2019.

15. WSJ.Insights, March 2016.

16. "Culture Quantified," WSJ.Insights, March 2016, partners.wsj.com, accessed May 30, 2016.

17. See Bourree Lam, "Why Are So Many Zappos Employees Leaving?," *The Atlantic*, January 15, 2016, theatlantic.com.

18. As faculty chair, heading up MBA program administration at the Harvard Business School, my motto, posted in classrooms and offices, was "We all learn. We all teach. For life."

19. Leonard L. Berry and Kent D. Seltman, *Management Lessons from Mayo Clinic: Inside One of the World's Most Admired Service Organizations* (New York: McGraw-Hill, 2008), 55.

20. Stefan H. Thomke, "Building a Culture of Experimentation," *Harvard Business Review*, March–April 2020, 48.

21. Nanette Byrnes, "The Art of Motivation," *Businessweek*, May 1, 2006, 57.

22. These relationships were first articulated in James L. Heskett, Thomas O. Jones, Gary W. Loveman, W. Earl Sasser Jr., and Leonard A. Schlesinger, "Putting the Service Profit Chain to Work," *Harvard Business Review*, March–April 1994, 164–174.

23. Robert S. Kaplan and David P. Norton, *The Balanced Scorecard* (Boston: Harvard Business School Press, 1996).

24. Schmidt, Rosenberg, and Eagle, *Trillion Dollar Coach*, 27–29.

25. Gifford Pinchot III, *Intrepreneuring: Why You Don't Have to Leave the Corporation to Become an Entrepreneur* (New York: Harper & Row, 1985), 138–139.

26. See *A Century of Innovation: The 3M Story* (St. Paul, MN: 3M Company, 2002), especially 38–40.

27. Much of this story is told in Thomas H. Davenport and Brook Manville, *Judgment Calls: 12 Stories of Big Decisions and the Teams That Got Them Right* (Boston: Harvard Business Review Press, 2012), 143–160.

28. Davenport and Manville, 148.

29. *LuvLines*, Southwest Airlines, February/March, 2001, 18.

APPENDIX: A ROBUST CULTURE-BASED BALANCED SCORECARD AUDIT

1. Robert S. Kaplan and David P. Norton, "The Balanced Scorecard: Measures That Drive Performance," *Harvard Business Review*, January–February 1992, 71–79.

INDEX

Page numbers in *italics* indicate figures or tables.

accountability: action and, 148–149; Coors prioritizing, 176; latitude and, 75; of leadership, 171; performance impacted by, 103; trust built by, 186; for values, 123

ACSI. *See* American Customer Satisfaction Index

action: accountability and, 148–149; behavior reinforced by, 202; communication of, 182; dissatisfaction and, 153; by leadership, 123, 169; measurement followed by, 125; organizational culture changed by, 149–150, *151*; performance necessitating, 154; with urgency, 157

agility, 21, 25

American Customer Satisfaction Index (ACSI), 42–43, 55

Anhorn, Sara, 130

arrogance: at Coors Brewing Company, 142; organizational culture and, 146; performance influencing, 15; profitability hurt by, 142

artifacts: behavior and, 37; culture ombudsman monitoring, 119; at Southwest Airlines, 229n5; values reflected in, 10

Automattic: Mullenweg founding, 233n7; remote work at, 134–135; technology at, 135

Babka, Richard Aldrich "Rink," 142–143

Beer, Michael, 153

behavior: action reinforcing, 202; artifacts and, 37; CEO demonstrating, 185; of leadership, 183, 197–198; organizational culture determined by, 173; strategy aligned with, 167; values and, 163, 208, 213–214. *See also* boundary-spanning behaviors

Benioff, Marc: on leadership, 32; on organizational culture, 5; on Salesforce, 5; on values, 30

Bogle, John: innovation by, 99; on stars, 205–206; in stories, 204–205; Vanguard Group led by, 99

Bossidy, Larry, 68

boundary-spanning behaviors: Nadella utilizing, 116; organizational culture aided by, 125

Bouven, Anders, 109–110

Brown, Linda, 206

burnout, 92–93

Burns, Ursula, 145

Caesar's Entertainment, 65

Campbell, Bill, 187

CEO: behavior demonstrated by, 185; of CM, 128–129; Ealy on, 158; Gerstner as, 184–185; Glassdoor rating, 94; IBM influenced by, 179–180; leadership of, 71, 88, 113; organizational culture led by, 4, 177, 191; as role models, 183–184; strategy controlled by, 179; T-Mobile led by, 72–73; Winterkorn and, 80–81

Charan, Ram, 68

Châteauform', 85

cheating: Gerstner on, 113–114; organizational culture influencing, 114–115; performance improved by, 112–113; symptoms and, 144; at Volkswagen, 23, 78–79; Winterkorn and, 79–81

Chesky, Brian, 76

Circuit City, 3

CM. *See* Critical Mass

Coca-Cola, 231n11

Collins, Jim, 178; on Circuit City, 3; on Kesey, 156; on leadership, 181

communication: action and, 182; organizational culture reshaped by, 155; of values, 165

community service: leadership encouraging, 118; in mission, 39–40; by Salesforce, 40, 117–118; teamwork and, 116–117; values communicated by, 117–118

compensation: for employees, 49; engagement and, 87; at Mayo Clinic, 110; organizational culture and, 13–14; Volkswagen paying, 80

competitive weapon, 9, 23, 26

conflict: Coors facing, 177; with diversity, 105; HBS managing, 115; with leadership, 114; teamwork reducing, 115

Coors, Peter: accountability prioritized by, 176; Babka with, 142–143; conflict faced by, 177; at Coors Brewing Company, 141–142; leadership by, 176; stories by, 177

Coors Brewing Company, 141–142
COVID-19 pandemic: agility in, 21,
    25; leadership in, 4–5; Liquid and,
    138; Osimek on, 233n5; remote
    work in, 127, 232n1; technology
    impacted by, 138
Critical Mass (CM): CEO of,
    128–129; organizational culture of,
    130–133; training at, 132. *See also*
    Liquid, by Critical Mass
Culture Cycle, The (Heskett), 234n1
culture ombudsman, 118–120
customer retention: engagement in,
    59–62, *60*, *62*, *212*, 216; at Ritz-
    Carlton, 86; values and, 228n11

Dalio, Ray, 11
Deloitte, 34
disruption, 72
dissatisfaction: action motivated by,
    153; Beer on, 153; at Microsoft,
    154; urgency and, 178
diversity: at Coca-Cola, 231n11;
    conflict with, 105; inclusion and,
    124; innovation enhanced by, 105;
    performance influenced by, 106;
    social justice and, 22; teamwork
    increased by, 105
Drucker, Peter, 225n15

Ealy, Tom, 158
Edmondson, Amy, 78, 171
employee engagement index (EEI),
    51
employees: compensation for, *49*;
    of MarketCo, 48, *49*; mission
    motivating, 38; organizational
    culture of, 22, 31; technology

challenging, 6; of TSA, 24. *See
    also* engagement, of employees
End of Competitive Advantage, The
    (McGrath), 18–20, *19*
engagement, of employees: with
    burnout, 92–93; compensation
    and, 87; in customer
    retention, 59–62, *60*, *62*, *212*,
    216; Gallup studying, 34, 53;
    growth influenced by, *212*; at
    Handelsbanken, 109; hiring for
    attitude and, 72, 96; leadership
    and, 23, 34–35, 43, 69, 75–76,
    88–89, 219; Legere impacting,
    190; organizational culture in,
    27, 99–100, 199; performance
    and, 42–43, 45–46, 211; Pfeffer
    on, 92; profitability and, 33,
    35, 42; recognition creating,
    90–91; recruitment and, 48, *49*;
    referrals through, 47–50, *49*, 66,
    122; relationships and, 55–59,
    58; in remote work, 133–134, 137;
    retention impacted by, 50–53,
    52, 227n4; returns influenced by,
    53–55, *54*; strategy overshadowing,
    31; talent development
    influencing, 81–82; teamwork
    impacted by, 215; technology
    increasing, 82–83; at T-Mobile,
    95; training for, 89–90; values and,
    82, 107; at Vanguard Group, 101
Epstein, Theo, 194
exit interviews, 93
experimentation: leadership
    encouraging, 108, 125; by Legere,
    180–181; performance improved
    by, 111

Fairbanks, Richard, 74
Francona, Terry, 194
Frei, Frances, 158
Friedman, Milton, 226n16
Fry, Art, 204–205
"Future of Remote Work, The"
    (Osimek), 233n5

Gallup: engagement studied by, 34,
    53; leadership studied by, 36
Gen Z, 82
Gerstner, Lou: as CEO, 184–185; on
    cheating, 113–114; IBM led by, 12;
    on organizational culture, 12, 179
Glass, David, 88
Glassdoor: ACSI with, 55; CEO
    rated by, 94; measurement by,
    55, 94; organizational culture
    measured by, 94
Greenleaf, Robert, 186
Grove, Andy, 14
growth: engagement influencing, 212;
    organizational culture influenced
    by, 32; profitability and, 56, 172;
    recruitment and, 229n6

Handelsbanken, 109
Harvard Business School (HBS),
    224n7; conflict managed at, 115;
    inclusion (for IBM) at, 106–107;
    leadership of, 100–101, 207;
    retention at, 98
Heskett, James, L., 234n1
hiring for attitude: engagement
    and, 72, 96; Fairbanks on, 74;
    by NYPD, 73–74; at Southwest
    Airlines, 74–75; with talent
    development, 214

Hobbes, Thomas, 144
Horowitz, Ben, 21
Houston, Drew, 161–162
HR. See human resources
Hsieh, Tony: on leadership, 28;
    with Madan, 27; middle
    management eliminated by, 195;
    on organizational culture, 11;
    stories of, 27
human resources (HR): cultural
    ombudsman compared with,
    120; Society of Human Resource
    Management as, 226; at Walmart,
    189–190

IBM: CEO influencing, 179–180;
    Gerstner leading, 12; Palmisano
    leading, 165; values of, 165
inclusion: of diversity, 124; at HBS,
    106–107; leadership prioritizing,
    105–106
ING Direct, 40–41
innovation: by Bogle, 99; diversity
    enhancing, 105; internal sharing
    and, 125; profitability influenced
    by, 64–65; trust increasing, 78
internal sharing: Bouven on, 109–110;
    innovation and, 125
Iverson, Ken, 12

Kalanick, Travis, 144
Kelleher, Herb, 12, 13, 188
Kesey, Ken, 156
Kotter, John, 15, 141, 148
Kuhlmann, Arkadi, 40–41

latitude, of employees: accountability
    and, 75; leadership giving, 84;

at Ritz-Carlton, 85–86; at
Southwest Airlines, 84
leadership: accountability of, 171;
action by, 123, 169; behavior
of, 183, 197–198; Benioff on,
32; building and, 1; burnout
fought by, 92–93; by Campbell,
187; CEO and, 71, 88, 113;
Châteauform' developing, 85;
Collins on, 181; community
service encouraged by, 118;
conflict with, 114; of Coors,
176; in COVID-19 pandemic,
4–5; Deloitte studying, 34;
engagement with, 23, 34–35,
43, 69, 75–76, 88–89, 219;
experimentation and, 108, 125;
Gallup studying, 36; of HBS,
100–101, 207; Hsieh on, 28;
inclusion prioritized by, 105–106;
latitude given to, 84; of Legere,
95; at Microsoft, 175; by middle
management, 136; mission
represented by, 213; of Muller,
79–80; by Odland, 169–170;
organizational culture and, 2, 13,
24–25, 110–111, 139, 182, 208, 209;
by Page, 203–204; performance
influenced by, 41, 99, 109–110,
179–180, 193; psychological
safety built by, 81–82;
recognition by, 86–87; stories on,
4, 204–205; strategy executed
by, 201–202; in symptoms, 145;
teaching recognized by, 196;
with technology, 3; trust in,
76–77, 79–80, 194; at Uber, 144;
with urgency, 24; values and,

80, 170, 176–178; at Vanguard
Group, 95; visibility of, 189; at
Walmart, 190; of Wells Fargo,
191–192; at Zappos, 195. See also
no-surprise leadership; servant
leadership
Legere, John: engagement impacted
by, 190; experimentation by,
180–181; leadership of, 95;
T-Mobile led by, 71, 180–181;
values prioritized by, 73
LinkExchange, 28–29
Liquid, by Critical Mass: COVID-
19 and, 138; talent development
in, 132. See also remote work
Lovelock, Christopher, 224n7

Madan, Sanjay, 27
MarketCo: in Chicago, 60;
employees of, 48, 49; profitability
of, 63; relationships of, 58; returns
of, 53–55, 54
Marriott, Bill, 184
Mayo Clinic: compensation at, 110;
organizational culture of, 101;
performance of, 99; stars at, 101
McGrath, Rita Gunther, 18–20, 19
measurement: action motivated
by, 125; by Glassdoor, 55, 94;
by middle management, 167;
of organizational culture,
166–167, 173–174, 199, 217–220,
224n9; of performance, 120–123,
171–172; of profitability, 218;
of recruitment, 226. See also
employee engagement index
(EEI); Glassdoor; Russell
index

Microsoft: dissatisfaction at, 154; leadership at, 175; Nadella leading, 16–17, 147–148, 153–154, 157, 159, 180; organizational culture of, 164; values of, 160–161

middle management: Hsieh eliminating, 195; leadership by, 136; Marriott emulated by, 184; measurement by, 167; remote work and, 136; training of, 140; trust in, 230n16; at Walmart, 90–91

millennials, 82–83

minority background individuals: at Coca-Cola, 231n11; social justice for, 5. *See also* diversity

mission: community service in, 39–40; employees motivated by, 38; leadership representing, 213; in organizational culture, 38–39, 44; profitability and, *212*; stories validating, 43; with strategy, 39

Mullenweg, Matt: Automattic founded by, 233n7; on remote work, 134

Müller, Matthew, 79–81

Nadella, Satya: boundary-spanning behavior utilized by, 116; Microsoft led by, 16–17, 147–148, 153–154, 157, 159, 180; organizational culture changed by, 160; on performance, 175; on SLT, 157; values prioritized by, 161

New York Police Department (NYPD), 73–74

nonbelievers, 195–196

no-surprise leadership, 193–195

Odland, Steve, 169–170

organizational culture: action changing, 149–150, *151*; arrogance and, 146; behavior determining, 173; Benioff on, 5; boundary-spanning behavior aiding, 125; CEO leading, 4, 177, 191; cheating influenced by, 114–115; of CM, 130–133; communication reshaping, 155; compensation and, 13–14; as competitive weapon, 9, 23, 26; EEI and, 51; of employees, 22, 31; in engagement, 27, 51, 99–100, 199; exit interviews improving, 93; Gerstner on, 12, 179; Glassdoor rating, 94; growth impacted by, 32; Horowitz on, 21; Houston on, 161–162; Hsieh on, 11; Kelleher on, 13; leadership and, 2, 13, 24–25, 110–111, 139, 182, 208, 209; at LinkExchange, 28–29; of Mayo Clinic, 101; measurement of, 166–167, 173–174, 199, 217–220, 224n9; of Microsoft, 164; millennials prioritizing, 82–83; mission with, 38–39, 44; Nadella changing, 160; nonbelievers damaging, 195; performance influenced by, 10–11, 14, 141, 143, 198, 200–201, *201*, 221; profitability with, *35*, 63–64, 66–68, *67*, 69; remote work influencing, 128, 132–133, 138–139; Russell index measuring, 11; scorecard audit of, 211, *212*; self-selection in, 124; stars hurting, 10–105; stories shaping, 1–2, 203, 208; strategy compared with, 9, 16–17, *19*, 20,

68–69, 150, 225n15; sustainability influenced by, 97; teamwork prioritized by, 103–105; in third industrial revolution, 6–7; of 3M, 228n12; training changing, 170; trust fostered by, 76, 121; urgency changing, 159; values defining, 29, 36–37, 65, 111, 156; at Wells Fargo, 112–113; Wilkins on, 128; in Zappos Culture Book, 101–102. *See also* symptoms, of problematic culture

Osimek, Adam, 233n5

Page, Larry, 203–204
Palmisano, Sam, 165
performance: accountability impacting, 103; action necessitated by, 154; arrogance influenced by, 15; cheating improving, 112–113; diversity influencing, 106; engagement and, 42–43, 45–46, 211; experimentation improving, 111; leadership influencing, 41, 99, 179–180, 193; leadership tracking, 109–110; of Mayo Clinic, 99; measurement of, 120–123, 171–172; Nadella on, 175; with nonbelievers, 196; organizational culture influencing, 10–11, 14, 141, 143, 198, 200–201, *201*, 221; profitability and, 46–47; Schmidt on, 11, 203–204; strategy and, 68; symptoms and, 150–152; trust and, 194; of values, 117, 168
Pfeffer, Jeffrey, 92
Phillips, Jean, 102

Pisano, Gary, 108
Pollard, Bill, 187
profitability: arrogance hurting, 142; engagement prioritizing, 33, *35*, 42; Friedman on, 226n16; growth and, 56, 172; innovation in, 64–65; of MarketCo, 63; measurement of, 218; mission and, *212*; organizational culture predicting, *35*, 63–64, 66–68, *67*, 69; performance and, 46–47
psychological safety: Edmondson on, 78, 171; leadership building, 81–82; trust and, 77–78, 96, 214; at Volkswagen, 78–79

recognition: engagement and, 90–91; by leadership, 86–87
recruitment: engagement and, 48, *49*; growth with, 229n6; measurement of, 226; Society of Human Resource Management measuring, 226
referrals, from employees: engagement and, 47–50, *49*, 66, 122; retention and, 216
relationship, with customers: engagement and, 55–59, *58*; of MarketCo, *58*; Salesforce forming, 39
remote work: at Automattic, 134–135; in COVID-19 pandemic, 127, 232n1; engagement in, 133–134, 137; middle management and, 136; Mullenweg on, 134; organizational culture influenced by, 128, 132–133, 138–139; Osimek studying, 233n5; retention

remote work (*continued*)
improved by, 137; teamwork and, 232n3; technology utilized by, 129, 133; Zuckerberg on, 127
retention, of employees: engagement impacting, 50–53, *52*, 227n4; at HBS, 98; referrals and, 216; remote work improving, 137
returns, to labor, 53–55, *54, 62*
Ritz-Carlton, 85–86
Rockport, 117
role models, 183–184
Russell index, 11

Salesforce: Benioff on, 5; community service by, 40, 117–118; relationship formed by, 39; stories at, 99–100; values of, 30
Schein, Edgar H., 16
Schmidt, Eric: on performance, 11, 203–204; stories by, 203–204; on talent development, 153
scorecard audit, of organizational culture, 211, *212*
self-selection: in organizational culture, 124; in United States Marine Corps, 100; values and, 102–103; at Zappos, 102
senior leadership team (SLT), 157
servant leadership: at ServiceMaster, 186–187; in United States Marine Corps, 186
ServiceMaster, 186–187
Sijbrandij, Sid, 135–136
Silver, Spencer, 204–205
Sloan, Tim, 191
SLT. *See* senior leadership team
social justice, 5, 22

Society of Human Resource Management, 226
Southwest Airlines: artifacts at, 229n5; Brown at, 206; hiring for attitude at, 74–75; Kelleher building, 12, 188; latitude at, 84; Lovelock on, 224n7; teamwork at, 103–104; 3M compared with, 12; values demonstrated by, 119, 187–188
stars: Bogle on, 205–206; at Mayo Clinic, 101; organizational culture hurt by, 104–105; teamwork damaged by, 103
stories: Bogle in, 204–205; by Coors, 177; of Hsieh, 27; on leadership, 4, 204–205; mission validated by, 43; organizational culture shaped by, 1–2, 203, 208; at Salesforce, 99–100; by Schmidt, 203–204; in training, 99–100; of United States Marine Corps, 97–98; values and, 206
strategy: behavior aligning, 167; CEO controlling, 179; engagement overshadowed by, 31; leadership executing, 201–202; mission with, 39; organizational culture compared with, 9, 16, 17, *19*, 20, 68–69, 150, 225n15; performance and, 68; Schein on, 16; values integrated by, 160
Streitfeld, David, 232n1
sustainability, 97
Swartz, Jeffrey, 117
symptoms, of problematic culture: Burns detecting, 145; cheating and, 144; leadership in, 145;

performance and, 150–152; at
Uber, 23; at Volkswagen, 78–79; at
Wells Fargo, 112–113

talent development: engagement
influenced by, 81–82; hiring for
attitude with, 214; in Liquid, 132;
Schmidt on, 153
teaching, 196
teamwork: community service
and, 116–117; conflict reduced
by, 115; diversity increasing,
105; engagement impacting,
215; organizational culture
prioritizing, 103–105; remote
work and, 232n3; at Southwest
Airlines, 103–104; stars damaging,
103; technology facilitating,
134–135; training influenced by,
104
technology: at Automattic, 135;
COVID-19 pandemic impacting,
138; disruption in, 72; employees
challenged by, 6; engagement
increased by, 82–83; Iverson on,
12; leadership with, 3; remote
work and, 129, 133; teamwork
facilitated by, 134–135
third industrial revolution, 6–7
Thomke, Stefan, 196–197
3M: organizational culture of, 228n12;
Southwest Airlines compared
with, 12; values at, 205
T-Mobile: CEO leading, 72–73;
engagement at, 95; Legere
leading, 71, 180–181
training, of employees: at CM,
132; for engagement, 89–90;

of middle management, 140;
organizational culture changed
by, 170; stories in, 99–100;
teamwork influencing, 104; of
United States Marine Corps,
97–98; at WIPRO, 90
Transportation Security
Administration (TSA), 24
trust: accountability building, 186;
Chesky on, 76; innovation
increased by, 78; in leadership,
76–77, 79–80, 194; in middle
management, 230n16; no-surprise
leadership encouraging, 193–195;
organizational culture fostering,
76, 121; performance and, 194;
psychological safety and, 77–78,
96, 214
TSA. See Transportation Security
Administration

Uber: Frei at, 158; leadership at, 144;
symptoms at, 23
United States Marine Corps:
self-selection in, 100; servant
leadership in, 186; stories of,
97–98; training of, 97–98
urgency: action with, 157;
dissatisfaction and, 178;
leadership with, 24;
organizational culture changed
by, 159

values: accountability for, 123;
Anhorn on, 130; artifacts
reflecting, 10; behavior and, 163,
208, 213–214; Benioff on, 30;
communication of, 165;

values (*continued*)
community service
communicating, 117–118; of
customer retention, 228n11;
engagement and, 82, 107; of IBM,
165; Kalanick contradicting,
144; leadership and, 80, 170,
176–178; Legere prioritizing, 73;
of Microsoft, 160–161; Nadella
prioritizing, 161; organizational
culture defined by, 29, 36–37,
65, 111, 156; performance of, 117,
168; Pollard reinforcing, 187; of
Salesforce, 30; self-selection and,
102–103; Southwest Airlines
demonstrating, 119, 187–188; story
and, 206; strategy integrating,
160; at 3M, 205
Vanguard Group: Bogle leading, 99;
engagement at, 101; leadership at,
95; Yu protecting, 205
Volkswagen: cheating at, 23, 78–79;
compensation paid by, 80; Müller

at, 80–81; psychological safety at,
78–79; symptoms at, 78–79

Walmart: Glass leading, 88; HR
at, 189–190; leadership at, 190;
middle management at, 90–91
Wells Fargo: leadership of, 191–192;
organizational culture at, 112–113;
Sloan on, 191; symptoms at,
112–113
Wilkins, Dianne, 128–129
Winterkorn, Martin: CEO and,
80–81; cheating and, 79–81
WIPRO, 90
World Series (2016), 194

Yu, Mabel, 205

Zappos: leadership at, 195; self-
selection at, 102; Zappos Culture
Book at, 101–102
Zappos Culture Book, 101–102
Zuckerberg, Mark, 127